The Trout and the Fly

D0745267

The Trout and the Fly
A NEW APPROACH

John Goddard and Brian Clarke

LYONS & BURFORD, PUBLISHERS

Copyright © 1980 by Brian Clarke and John Goddard

ALL RIGHTS RESERVED. No part of this book may be
reproduced in any manner without the express written
consent of the publisher, except in the case of brief excerpts
in critical reviews and articles. All inquiries should be
addressed to: Lyons & Burford, 31 West 21 Street, New
York, NY 10010.

Printed in the United States of America

10 9 8 7 6 5 4 3 2 1

Library of Congress Catalog Card Number: 84-60419
ISBN: 1-55821-113-6

To the trout, to the water, to the sunlight and the sky, and to the stillness of the meadow in the evening

Contents

List of numbered illustrations

All the photographs in this book were taken by the authors, except those showing how the new flies are dressed, and those few specifically noted in the acknowledgements.

Introduction to the American edition

Misinformation on trout fishing, like the sins of the fathers, seems to be passed down from generation to generation. Most fly-fishing books for decades have tended either to repeat and reinforce what previous "authorities" have written or to offer minor variations blown up as new theories.

Brian Clarke and John Goddard have broken out of this vicious circle and started from scratch. All the premises and practices put forth in *The Trout and The Fly* are based on visual evidence of what trout actually do—not what anglers *think* they do.

The authors may be little known in America up to now, but they are already legends in England. They have spent years observing trout resting, fleeing, and, especially, feeding to solve many fly-fishing puzzles. They show you not only how to find and observe trout yourself, but how the behaviour of individual trout furnishes solid information on which fly to use and how to present it. Do not hastily protest that you are an angler, not a voyeur. This is the most fascinating, eye-opening section of a pioneering book. If you practise what the authors preach on your stream—even though it may differ from English waters—you will become a far more effective and rewarded angler. And you may be well on your way to making significant discoveries of your own.

All Clarke–Goddard theories have been tested and re-tested during several seasons on many rivers and over large, jaundiced trout—not stockers or wilderness innocents. New fly dressings have been compared with standard ones under special underwater observation conditions as well as on trout. Trout biology and optics have been fully researched and the experts consulted. The result is a startlingly new approach to trout fishing.

Before you start the book proper, try this true/false test. After you've finished reading, return to these questions and check how many of your original answers were off the mark. I think you'll be chagrined.

Big trout seldom feed in shallow riffles. Most trout prefer to lie behind, rather than in front of obstacles. A trout can focus sharply on an object within one inch of its nose. The color most visible to trout is yellow. Wings on dry flies imitating duns are excessive baggage—body color is more important. Dubbed fur or herl are the best available body materials for dry flies. The floating fly line color least visible to trout is white. During a glut hatch of mayflies, dead drift is the best presentation. You should cast a nymph so that it enters the water as silently as possible.

As you can tell from the topics covered, this is a high-protein book, indeed, and yet the meat is amply garnished. The authors wield the language with precision and grace—their prose sparkles. Even their most factual and scientific passages are a joy to read and re-read.

And re-read it you will. I have just completed my third reading, and I know I will return again. I envy you who are picking up this book for the first time. The first trip through is high adventure.

Leonard M. Wright, Jr
New York
August 1979

Acknowledgements

We have had a great deal of help from others in the preparation of this book, and wish in particular to record our thanks to the following:

First and foremost to that master fly-dresser Stewart Canham, who made up our one-thousand-and-one experimental fly-dressing designs that they might be field-tested by ourselves and others. His good humour and professionalism carried him through a series of amendments, alterations and retyings that would have reduced a lesser man to despair; and he put himself to numerous other inconveniences on our behalf.

Professor W.R.A. (Bill) Muntz, of the Department of Biology, Stirling University, for sharing with us some of his rare knowledge of fish vision, and for preparing for us (twice!) the fascinating chart which appears in the chapter "How the Trout Sees".

Dr Ray Shack and Dr Ruth Fenn, physicists both, who guided us patiently through the labyrinths of underwater optics; and Bob Adams, our friendly neighbourhood lecturer in mathematics, who checked our various sums.

Ron Clark, the Darryl F. Zanuck behind the camera for the remarkable sequence "A Leviathan Falls".

Max King, who provided an invaluable pair of hands during some of our experiments, and who gave professional help in our measurement of light angles.

Barry Woodward and Dennis Mutton for their forbearance during our experimentation on the Wilderness, the Benham Estate's stunning water on the Kennet; and the fishery's omnipresent keeper, Bernard James.

Mr Seton Wills, for similarly allowing us unrestricted access to his excellent water at Littlecote on the Upper Kennet for the purpose of observation and experiment; and his helpful and knowledgeable keepers, Don Macer Wright and Peter Woolnough.

Roy Darlington, for his continuing kindness in allowing us to fish and observe on his historic water at Abbotts Barton on the Itchen.

The Sunday Times, London, and its photographer Mark Ellidge, for permission to reproduce the photograph of BC on page 151.

Dick Pobst, of the Keel Fly Company of America, and his UK agents H. Turrall, for their help in tracing and obtaining the many hooks we experimented with; and Dermot Wilson of Nether Wallop Mill, who was similarly helpful.

Ted Andrews, artist, who converted our (somewhat) rough illustrations into the line drawings that appear in the following pages; and Jonathan Newdick, designer, who conceived the cover design and laid out every single page of the text. Both were unfailing in their cooperation.

Marion Buckwell and Margaret Gaillot, who typed our manuscript.

Our many fishing friends – and in particular our fellow-rods – for their companionship and their constant willingness to discuss experiences.

And finally (because they are so important) our wives. Greater fortitude hath no woman, than she who marries both fisherman and writer, simultaneously.

Prologue: the trout and the fly

More books have been written about the trout than about any other fish, and perhaps even any other animal; and more books have been written about fly-fishing than about any other branch of the angler's art.

What is it about the trout and the fly, that fascinates so?

Certainly, in the case of the trout, it is not his size. There are many fish that grow bigger than he; and anglers, in any event, make few distinctions between trout of different sizes: it is not *absolute* size that is important to the angler; it is – where it is a factor at all – *relative* size: the size of the fish we want or have caught, compared to other fish in the water. A half-pound trout from an upland stream can give every bit as much pleasure in its way, as does a 2 lb trout from a rich lowland river, or a 5 lb trout from a lake.

If it is not his size, then is it his intelligence? Is the trout endowed with wits beyond his kind? Has he a brain to match our own; to parry and thrust as we plot and scheme?

No, it is hardly his intelligence. The trout is not intelligent, even for a fish. How could he be caught on flies at all, how could he – given his excellent sight – be so terminally indiscriminating, if he were intelligent?

Then what? If it is obviously not his intelligence and his size, then what can it be that allures so? His beauty?

Well, certainly the trout is a beautiful creature. He is exquisitely streamlined; a poem to the eye as he throbs on the current, with the waters sleeking by him like liquid, silent time. And his colouring is spectacular, too, painted by the Master's hand; now gold and olive, now blue and silver, now mottled with red spots and black; the most delicate brushwork on a glistening sheen. So – yes, his beauty must be a factor.

And what else? His fight? Yes, again – certainly his fight. The trout – in particular the trout with a current to help him – is the most volatile fish that swims.

That is not to say he is the most dogged, or the most powerful: in England, the carp and the barbel are both stronger than he: but they are not as dashing. And above all, perhaps, they do not leap. They do not break that barrier of the water surface, to show themselves in elemental and outraged beauty, in the manner of the trout. They do not, with that single thrust of the tail, leap not simply into our sight, but like some glistening lance, clearly into the mind in arrested detail.

Who cannot see it now? The line lengthening and lengthening as he nears the surface, and as the reflections above him distort, and then rock. In a shaving off a second, a fragment off time, he is not there and then he is, in lightning slow motion: in cinematographic frames that will play back as dreams long after the summer has gone.

Images. The arch of his body painted on afternoon air; water, drawn up from his tail in a quicksilvered skirt, a membrane mirror stretched beyond the point of pain, and bursting like shattered mosaic; spray, like crystals impaled upon sunbeams. The glimpse of a cocked-white eye, sightless in the impervious air, and the fly, feathered Judas, clicked in the corner of his jaw, with the pink of his mouth inside. And then the crash; the plume of water as he

11

re-enters *his* world, before walking on his tail, down an eddy. Oh yes, the fight and the leap are important factors in the fascination of the trout.

And there is something else. His rise – again, that breaking of the barrier between him and us. The gleam of sunlight on camouflaged flank; magic, ebbing rings. *Pure* magic. They wrench the attention, they magnetize the eye, in a way that the feeding habits of other fishes never do. They draw the mind down into that silent void, pull the mind down into his mysterious, liquid womb.

And it is not just the rise, per se, but the wonderful variety of his rise, as well. The most delicate, subliminal sip: so delicate, sometimes, that it can't have happened, can't have happened, *did* it? And the slash – violent, furious, predatory, a challenge splashed high in the air. And the roll, oiled and languid from broad dark shoulder to sun-shot tail.

Yes, his rise is a factor, too; an important factor. And there are many other considerations, besides: perhaps as many attractions to the trout as there are anglers who fish for him.

Perhaps an even more interesting question, though, is not why the trout should command affection so, but why the *fly*? Why is this curious code embraced? *Why* have such esoteric limitations on the catching of a fish, been handed from father to son, from country to country until now, throughout much of the world, the "only" way to pursue the trout, for millions, is with feathered confections on hooks?

We do not – do we? – impose the code of *imitation* on the pursuit of other fish, as a point of ethics and pride. The world is not populated by men and women who drift floating "bread" of cotton wool, to carp as the light goes down; or by matchmen who lie abed at night devising new dressings of the larva of the bluebottle, with which to deceive their quarry. *They* use the real thing, we *imitate* – with all of the complications which that involves.

Of course, we *do* add to the sport by accepting the fly: and not just in difficulty, either. Fly-dressing is almost a pursuit on its own; and for some, fly-casting is an interest even where there are no fish.

But it is not these things about the fly, and the problems and diversities which it presents, that make fly-fishing the fascination that it is. They may be important for some, but they are effects and not the cause.

There are, like the trout itself no doubt, as many fascinations about the fly as there are men who fish it. At the heart of them all, we believe there are four that are of special importance. The first and the third are considerations that apply to other forms of angling, though in a less distilled and direct way; the others are fly-fishing's own.

The first consideration, we believe, is that man is a natural hunter, and that fly-fishing – particularly fly-fishing on rivers – gives him an opportunity to *stalk* his quarry, as he did before memory began. Other branches of angling are hunting, too: but few give the opportunity to hunt *specific* fish. The fly enables the angler to act out, in more than a mannered way, some elemental trace of the forest and glade that lies within us all.

The second reason, we suggest, why the fly is so attractive, is that it draws the fish up from his position in the water, and causes him to make the breathtaking rise that we have already discussed. And in causing his quarry to rise, it enables the angler not simply to deceive it by cunning but to see the moment of deception; to witness the consummation of his skills.

The third consideration is that the moment of the "take" is utterly direct: him there, us here, joined simply by the line and the rod, down into our feeling hands.

We react not to a float that intervenes, nor to the movement of a weight which deadens, but to him, at once. There is nothing at all to dilute the contact. Only the drifted bait compares in other forms of angling; and only the *floated* drifted bait, enables the take itself to be seen in a similar way.

And so to the fourth consideration: one that is fly-fishing's own; one that concerns "the bait".

One of the reasons that the fly has the following it enjoys, we believe, is because of the very *absence* of "bait". And one of the reasons why men have devoted so many of their energies to solving the problems of the fly, is because the problems that the fly presents are *aesthetic* problems: problems that lead immediately to clean, aesthetic solutions or else to more aesthetic problems. Problems (and we write as men who have fished for all manners of fish in all manners of ways, with all manners of baits both dead and alive) that do not involve *mess* in their preparation. There are no buckets of goo and slices of gore; no baskets and bins to burden our approach.

The fly is a physically clean device; one that lends itself to delicacy, mobility and lightness. And like us, we believe, other fly-fishers are glad of the fact. So the fly, among all its many other blessings, lends *elegance* to the pursuit of trout.

Let us now look at each of the two – at the trout and his fly – more closely.

In the looking, let us remember that we are not setting out to study English trout in English rivers, or American trout in American rivers, or New Zealand's trout in New Zealand's rivers. While circumstances may change in the specific – for example the river may be clearer or more opaque, or be wider or deeper – the basic facts with which we are concerned, have a common denominator from which all else flows; and it is that common denominator with which we are here concerned.

A trout is a trout is a trout; and his life is governed by the same series of needs and laws, *wherever he swims*.

PART ONE

Observation

Man and trout

1 The approach

To learn much about the trout in clear-water streams it is necessary, first of all, to get close enough to see him. But as the more experienced angler knows, to see a fish in clear water before he sees you – particularly in conditions of flat light in high summer – can be easier said than done. A sudden movement, a careless break of cover, an inappropriate choice of clothing, will send the trout bow-waving towards the Antipodes in terror, or sinking softly to the bottom like some half-remembered dream.

There are many ingredients of an unsuspected approach to the trout. All of them rest upon basic commonsense, and yet few of them are practised by most anglers on the bankside, and all of them are practised by very few fishermen indeed, that we see.

It is important that these ingredients are understood *now*, at the beginning of this tactical treatise. If they are not, or are not acted upon, then most of what else follows will prove academic.

Clothing

Make sure that your clothes match the predominant kind of background against which you will be working. If the banks are mostly wooded or steep, wear dull greens and browns. If the banks are low or devoid of cover, realize that it is a nonsense to wear a camouflaged jacket: wear a light blue or light green shirt. If you are fishing against contrasts of light – for example, against a background of sparse woodland – it is a good plan to break up your own colour profile by wearing, say, a green or green-and-brown fishing waistcoat over a rather lighter or darker shirt.

Movement

The golden rule on the riverbank is – move slowly. And move *smoothly*. The man who wishes to see the trout before it sees him, moves *softly*, as well. He does not stamp on the bank, or kick stones over, or stand on boughs that are likely to snap, or trudge noisily over gravel and stony reaches, to get to the waterside. He picks his way. He also carries his arms low down, and moves them as little as he must. He carries his rod low down, too – and behind him for safety. He does not turn his head unnecessarily, or abruptly from side to side, particularly if he is wearing spectacles that can act like a heliograph. (And if he is fishing, he makes sure that his rod does not act like a heliograph, too, by coating it in matt varnish, and not the spectacular gloss.) And there is another thing: when he has reached a likely piece of water, he will stand still, and wait and watch for many minutes on end. By doing so, he will give himself a chance of seeing those fish that spend most of their time under weeds and rocks, but that occasionally drift out from them. He will have the opportunity of seeing the arrival of trout recently departed upon protracted beats, or returning from alternative lies. And he will see much of the purring, furry, feathered, bright-eyed life of the riverside, too: the life that lends charm to his fishing.

Fig. 1 A pattern of approach, when bankside cover is sparse. The dotted lines indicate the water scanned from different positions. Between patches of cover drop back from the waterside, and walk only close enough to it to give you sight of the distant and middle water. Carefully done, this will save disturbance of the fish close to the bank. Only when the far water has been scanned should an approach be made right up to the water edge—either behind cover or (where cover is not available) crouched low or on hands and knees. Study the close-up water upstream and down, from this position.

Cover

Use every scrap of cover that the Good Lord (or a good fishery manager) has given you. If there is no cover, walk as far back from the bank as is consistent with seeing into most of the likely water, and look as far upstream as you clearly can. If you have to walk across a high skyline between clumps of trees, keep low, and keep back. It is often worth sacrificing a few yards of water altogether, rather than risk the spooking of a trout that would probably see you, and that might rush upstream to spook others that would not have.

If there are trees at intervals along an open bank, walk as far back from the bank edge as you sensibly can, and only approach the water when covered by one of them: come up behind it crouched low or on hands and knees, and do *not* stand up until you are close enough to the tree to put your arms around its trunk (Fig. 1). When you do stand up, stand up very slowly. When you have stood up, study the water downstream that you have just passed, and the water opposite. Then study the water upstream, that you are about to by-pass. Repeat the process at each tree. If there are bankside sedges, do not break them down along the water's edge to get a better view: you may need them again; you will have eroded the beauty of the riverside; and, almost inevitably, what started out as a footpath will end up as a motorway.

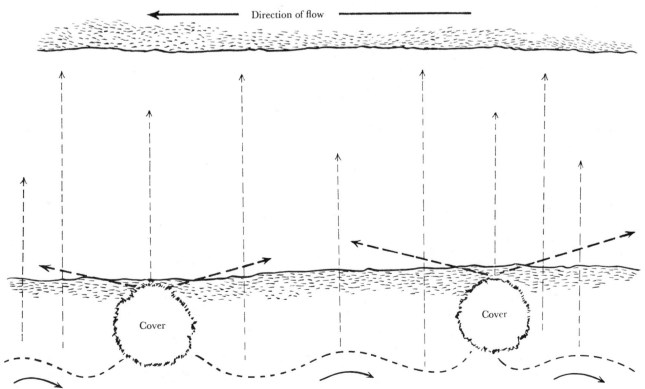

Direction of flow

Cover

Cover

Wading

Wading, where it is allowed, can be a useful ploy: it can take you nearer to the fish; it can enable you to approach directly from behind, to take advantage of his one real blind spot; it can, at its most simple, get you off a skyline. But be warned. Wading is on a par with sudden movement as a means of scaring trout. So never wade unless it will give you a distinct advantage; and if you do wade, *move with the utmost care*. Clumsy wading – studded boots shovelled across rocks on the bottom, felt boots forced down between two rocks causing one of them to roll over – will greatly reduce the chances of your fish still being there, when you get anywhere near his lie.

There is one thing you can do when wading, however, more than any of these, that will effectively cause your trout to bolt: you can create a bow-wave to surge off the prow of your waders, as you move.

On a river, a surge of water upstream is likely to kill your approach to a nearby fish, at any time. But on a bright day, on broad river shallows or lakeside margins, surges of water ahead of you, will disturb trout far beyond the range of your underwater vision. The disturbance does not have to be violent. On a sunny day even a slight ripple on the surface can be transformed into a rolling, blinking semaphore, as a broad ring of sunlight pulses across the bottom beneath every surface crinkle.

Wade when you must. *We* do not hesitate to wade where it is allowed, when it will give us an advantage.

But wade with care – smoothly, with great patience. And again, wade *only when it is necessary*: even a small amount of wading can do a great deal of damage to the aquatic life of the riverbed; and on a lake, it can so deplete the marginal feed that it drives the fish further and further from the shore. Indeed, on stillwaters we would be very happy to see wading banned completely.

Why are trout happy to lie in front of obstacles to the current on rivers, apparently in the full force of the flow? (See "Where Trout Lie".) This photograph shows the reason clearly. When the current strikes an object in its path, its progress is halted, and a "pad" or "cushion" of slower water is created. It is on this comfortable cushion that the trout rides, with very little expenditure of effort. The cushion in front of each of the supports of this footbridge is made clearly visible in low evening light.

2 How to see trout

In setting out to observe the trout, two related points need to be borne in mind. The first is that he is not going to be easy to see; the second is that given reasonable light, clarity of water, and a little knowledge and effort, he *can* be seen.

We should not be surprised that seeing the trout in his own environment is not going to be an easy business. The trout has not evolved to make himself easy to see, for predators on wing, fin or feet. He has evolved to make himself difficult to see; and the fact that he has survived so long, and is so widely distributed, is eloquent testimony to his success.

In the proving-grounds of evolution, he has learned all manner of tricks to make himself difficult to see. He is, for example, not simply born with a coloration which marries him to his native river: he will change colour (and has been observed to make the change in a matter of days) to take on the appropriately camouflaging hues, when transferred to a different water.

More specifically, the trout often adopts a camouflage custom-designed to a specific reach *and even lie*.

If he frequents a beat lined with bright gravel and sand, he may gleam like morning gold. If he inhabits the deeper water, or a pool that has long been silted up, he will be many shades darker on the back. If he inhabits the crisp, fresh-laundered runs between weedbeds on alkaline streams, he will often be bright silver, like the sea-trout. BC has seen many trout on heavily weeded streams that had heavy pigmentations of olive green. JG has even seen trout with dark, vertical, perch-like stripes on their sides as a direct result, he believes, of living in close proximity to reeds growing up through the water.

So there are no grounds at all for expecting the trout to be easy to see.

But that does not mean we need eyes like lasers, in order to see him. We know men of technically modest sight, who see more fish than most; and G.E.M. Skues, it is comforting to note, saw well enough with a single eye, to found a new branch of the visual, fly-fishing arts.

It is our experience that in the matter of seeing the trout in his element, it is not eyesight that transcends all else. The ability to spot the trout consistently, hinges upon several factors. The first is knowing how to make the best use of what eyesight we have been given – *how* to look; the second lies in knowing *what* to look *for*; and the third, in knowing *where* to look.

In this chapter, and those that immediately follow it, we will look at each of these factors in turn. But before we do, let us raise a fourth consideration; *practice*. Practice in seeing fish – particularly practice with a companion who himself knows how to see them – is very important indeed. It will enable you to improve your powers of observation, no matter what stage they might hitherto have reached.

The eyes

Few fishermen (or indeed, anyone else) give much thought to the most important consideration in seeing anything: the amount of light which reaches the eyes.

In looking for the trout in his environment, we are going to be looking for very subtle indications indeed that he is present. For this reason, we need to admit to the eye as much of the important light (which is to say, light from the water area into which we are looking) as we can; and conversely, we need to cut off from the eye as much unimportant light (light from areas into which we are not looking) as we are able.

The first physical aid we can give our eyes, that will enable them to perform their critical role better, will be something to cut out the glare of the sky. One way that this can be achieved, is by the simple expedient of wearing a wide-brimmed or long-peaked hat; another is the use of a linen-backed eyeshade of the type used by some tennis players, golfers, and spectators of outdoor sports (Fig. 2).

Fig. 2 Two hit-men from the Mafia. Left, JG in the peaked cap he uses to keep the sun from his eyes and (right) BC in the eyeshade that he prefers. The Polaroids we are wearing are standard aids when observing fish, or when attempting to catch them on nymph.

The second physical help we can give to the eyes is a pair of polarized spectacles to reduce surface reflections. All reflections manage to do – as we shall discuss in a moment – is to prevent the eye from piercing the surface film.

In choosing your polarized spectacles, do not make the mistake of trying to combine "sunglasses" with "seeing" glasses. Sunglasses have no place in "seeing" fishing. They simply reduce the amount of light coming to the eye: and it is light – light from the water in which the fish reside – that you want.

*Buy the clearest polarized spectacles you can find.**

You can, incidentally, improve the usefulness of polarized spectacles on a given stretch of water, by rotating them slightly on your nose. In one position they'll cut out one plane of light, enabling you to see into one part of the river; in another position, they'll cut out other areas of reflection, and enable you to

*It is a small point but if you are shopping for polarized lenses, and you're not sure that those on the counter have been so treated – simply hold one pair of glasses in front of another, and rotate them in opposite directions. If, in looking through one to the other, the lenses appear to go dark, or almost black, then they're both polarized. If they do not appear to go dark, then at least one set of lenses is not polarized.

see down into new water. (Of such fine dodges as these are successful fishermen made!)

Using the light

The most favourable conditions for seeing into the water occur on windless days when the sun is either behind the shoulders or immediately overhead.

Conversely, the worst conditions occur in high winds, when the surface becomes rippled, and on cloudy days, when the surface throws back a uniform, impenetrable grey. When there is a ripple, it becomes impossible to see into the water at all. In conditions of much cloud, the only real hope of seeing into the water is by gaining a vantage point high above the surface. For this reason, on these occasions, maximum use should be made of high banks with cover behind them; and of rocks, logs and other bankside furniture which can be stood upon to give a higher perspective, when there is cover behind.

On the sunny day, few problems are likely to be presented from late morning until early afternoon. Depending, however, upon the time of year and the bank being fished, there is unlikely to be some time when the sun is not ahead of you, and the water has not taken on its silvered sheen.

When it does, there are several things that you can do, to alleviate the problem.

The first, of course, is again to take advantage of the bankside furniture, to gain a higher perspective: at least that way you will gain some insight to the water under your own bank.

A second and more comprehensive approach is to seek out, if it is available to you, a stretch of river that is lined on the far bank with trees: their reflections will remove the sheen, and enable you to see down through the surface without trouble.

A third measure you can employ, if the banks are mostly open, is to seek out a single tree or bush on the opposite bank, and glue your eyes to its reflection, as slowly you walk your own side of the river. Again, its single reflection will cut out the glare – and will follow you around, as you move. In effect, it gives you a moving vertical line that is reflection-free, enabling you to scan the water little by little (Fig. 3).

Movement and concentration

When, either because the day is right or you have adopted one of the ploys above, you are in a position from which you can see into the water – stand still. Water cannot be scanned thoroughly when you are on the move at the trot.

As you move, so your perspective on objects changes; as you move, so they change shape; as you move, so they move in relation to other objects which may themselves (for example, weedbeds) be moving. And in looking for all the subtleties of light, and shape, and movement that the camouflaged trout is going to present to us, it makes no sense to volunteer for handicaps.

Fig. 3 How the reflection of a tree (or any other large object on the opposite bank) can cut out the surface glare and enable the fly-fisherman to see down into the water, as he walks along the bank.

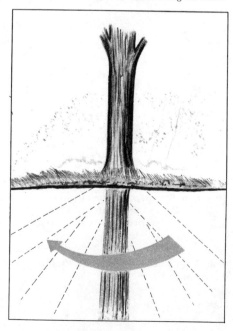

So – stand still, and concentrate. Do not concentrate *on* the water, concentrate on a depth and an area *in* the water. And bring your willpower into play. Resolve that if fish are there, then you will see them: like so much else in life, seeing fish if they are there to be seen at all, is an attitude of mind.

If experience tells you that the stretch of water you are looking at is "holding" water, and you see one fish, do not rest your investigation there. The odds are that if the water looks good, and it can be seen to hold one trout, then it will hold others. Look for the rest before you resort to any kind of action: the one you haven't seen will be the one you spook; and by that quaint angling law that we know so well, it will be the biggest of the bunch, as well.

And there is something else. Remember the effect of light upon the eye. If you've gone to the trouble of wearing an eyeshade or a hat to allow your pupils to open and admit more light, do not waste the advantage which that gives you. Do not, for example, range your eyes from dark, to light, to dark. All that you'll achieve will be to cause the pupils to contract when you look at the light and cause them to stay temporarily contracted when they look back at the dark.

As a result, very little will have been gained from your hat or your eyeshade; and very little will have been seen, as well. *When looking for trout, address the shaded areas first from your stationary position, and then address the areas of light.*

And when you move from areas of light to areas of dark, give your eyes time to adjust.

What to look for (general)

Knowing what to look for, is the Catch 22 of seeing fish: you're lucky if you see fish without knowing what to look for; but you don't really know what to look for, until you've learned to recognize fish.

Of course, if that were literally and absolutely true, dictionaries would lose much of their value as aids to spelling. We could not pick up a dictionary to check the spelling of a word, because to look the word up in a book arranged in alphabetical order, we would first need to know the sequence in which the letters occurred.

But just as we manage with dictionaries, so we can manage with trout, given some determination, commonsense, and sensitivity.

The question of seeing trout can be likened to the principles of "computer matching". With a little experience, we can imprint upon the mind's eye what we might expect to see; and when the picture recorded by the eyes matches the image imprinted upon the mind, then the brain registers "fish"!

The analogy encapsulates perfectly the problem of those who set out to find fish, and fail to see them even when fish are there. They have imprinted upon their minds the images of fish, and then gone off in search of a visual image to match their mental image.

Almost the *last* thing that the experienced observer looks for is a fish – or at least a *whole* fish. He looks for parts of fish, indications of fish, hints of fish, winks and suggestions of fish, as set out below.

As will become clear shortly one of the most common indications of a trout is its tail: not the whole fish, not the rear half of the fish; not even the shape of a clearly-defined tail; simply the throbbing, rhythmic shadow that the tail suggests, pulsing in the water.

The experienced man will have "tail rhythms" clearly fixed among his mental images; and when his eyes see that metronome's shadow, his brain registers "tail" and then the "fish!" bell rings. When the inexperienced man has a mental image of a fish – or even a tail as he is accustomed to seeing it – and his eyes arrive at that throbbing shade, his brain does not register a match, and he does not perceive the trout.

Frank Sawyer, in his historic book *Nymphs and the Trout*, gives a graphic illustration of the mind of a master observer at work; and the clearest demonstration of the matching process.

Sawyer recalls that often when he has been looking for pike to trap, he has failed to see trout, even though they have been lying in open positions; and conversely, that when he has been looking for trout, he has failed to see pike.

In the case of Sawyer his mental image was so refined that he wasn't looking for a visual match to hints of a mental "fish", he was looking for a visual match to hints of a mental species of fish. Very few anglers indeed, reach that degree of sophistication!

What to look for (specific)

Physical clues to the presence of fish fall into two broad and often overlapping categories: movements; and shadows and shapes. Before setting out to perceive them, there is one essential preparation: to "read yourself into" each stretch of water, as you come to it.

Every reach of every river has its own features: weedbeds, large rocks, undulating pebble banks, gullies, pots, shallows and deeps; and each has its own character too; a "personality" that is the product of some or all of these features, and the current's reaction to them. Study this "character" of the water, first, and understand what you can expect to see. There is no magic involved: the current and the riverbed furniture show what you can expect to see: it is what is there.

When the pattern of events, the interplays of light and contortions of the current, are clearly imprinted upon your mind begin, then, to look for *anything different or foreign*; anything out of place; anything that draws the eye twice to any piece of water as it presents itself.

In looking for the foreign and the unusual, have imprinted upon your mind, the following.

Movements

The greatest betrayer of prey to predator is movement.

Camouflage – as we have already discovered – is a magnificent device that is found everywhere in the animal kingdom. It is designed to merge an otherwise naked creature into its background. But backgrounds do not move; or at least, they do not transport themselves from one place to another, even though elements of them may bend and sway in collective response to winds and currents.

It is because backgrounds do not physically transport themselves that camouflaged creatures, almost without exception, "freeze" when danger approaches. The very absence of flight is a protective mechanism.

The protection goes when movement begins, as any stooping hawk or hunting cat will tell you.

And so it is with the trout. Perhaps the most common factor that betrays the trout is its movement. So imprint this upon your mind: *movement equals fish*.

There are many kinds of movement. Perhaps the most common of all the give-aways, as we have already discussed, is the pulse of the trout's tail, in the current: a throbbing shadow with (sometimes) a clean, vertical, trailing edge.

It is extraordinary that one can see the pulse of the tail, without being able to see the whole fish first; but be assured that it is so. Be assured, as well, that this is the essence of "matching".

A second kind of movement to be alert for is a flash of light from below water, caused by the abrupt turn of a fish and the reflection of the sunlight from its flank. Yet another signal is the blink of white from the mouth of a trout, as it takes a nymph. It may sound unbelievable that such a tiny movement can be seen – but we assure you that it is so (see picture on page 81). A third type of tell-tale movement is the one that is, for want of a better term, "out of synch" with the other movements we can see or expect to see, in the river.

Give or take the odd eddy and whorl, the movement of the water is downstream; and everything that is floating free in the water, or is growing up into it from the bottom, reflects the fact. So look for:

1. Anything which suggests movement upstream, against the current;
2. Anything which drops downstream in a controlled way; or which drops downstream and then stops;
3. Anything which is moving in one direction, when the current is rhythmically wafting weed in another;
4. Anything which appears to drift from one weedbed to another, and does not move back again in harmony with the movements of the vegetation (Fig. 4).

It is worth stressing again that you are not looking for a fish-shape doing these things: you are looking for anything at all doing these things: it may be a dark shadow, it may be a light reflection; it may be something light *and* dark, or something dark upon dark or light upon light. It is any kind of foreign movement, that you are looking for.

Do not always expect to see something physical moving *in* the water. Look for changes in the movement of the water itself. Again, the movement of the current is in a downstream direction; and a moment or two spent in observation of the surface convolutions will show what the eye can expect to

perceive. When that "normal" base of information has been stored in the mind, look a minute or two longer. Very often, it will be possible to see momentary changes of the water surface, as the current reacts to the movement of an unseen fish.

In rippled water (see "Locating Invisible Fish") look for a local patch of ripple in which the wavelets move broadside to the general current. In smooth water look for regularly shaped reflections that become irregular and for sharp reflections that suddenly blur. Imprint all of these phenomena upon your mind, and imprint "fish!" upon your mind, beside them.

Fig. 4 A clear patch in the middle of a weedy stretch . . . and a fleeting glimpse of a big trout as it drifts lazily from one side of the opening to the other. It is such brief glimpses as this (the shadowy outline of the trout in the centre of the clearing was gone in less than a second!) that make all the difference to a day's success.

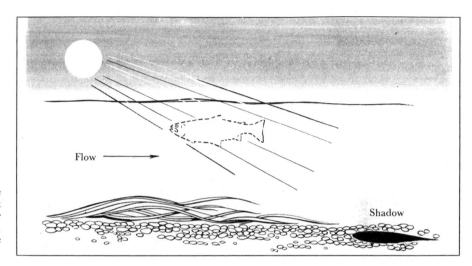

Fig. 5 How a shadow on the bottom can reveal the true position of a fish lying elsewhere. In bright sunlight, draw a mental line through the water between the shadow on the bottom, and the sun. The fish that you are seeking, will lie somewhere along that line.

Shadows and shapes

Shadows are an important register in the mental gallery of the fish-watcher. They come in all kinds, and bear all manner of significances. Two are worth a special mention, because they introduce the need for caution.

The first – and one of the most difficult to see – is that produced by a fish lying in deep water; in particular, by the fish lying in a deep pot, in the middle of a shallow reach.

The trout that lies in a deep pool spends most of his time close to the bottom, because it is safer there. He will be a shadow upon a shadow; or just occasionally, if he is newly-arrived, a marginally lighter shade than that of the dark bottom upon which he lies.

If such a fish sees you before you see him, you may spend fruitless minutes trying to do him wrong. Such a fish will not bolt when he is alarmed: he will simply sink deeper down onto the bottom, pressing himself almost upon it; putting as much distance between you and his good self, as he can. He knows you are there; he knows you know he is there. It is stalemate. You must approach the water with caution.

The second shadow that is worth special mention occurs on gravelled bottoms, in shallower water, on sunny days. It is a shadow, for once, that looks quite like a fish.

Never cast to a shadow such as this, in the conditions described, without careful observation, first. You may, of course, cast if you wish; but often enough you'll be there till Doomsday and some way beyond, before you come near to inducing a take.

The reason is that this shade is often not a fish at all, but a genuine shadow: and the fish that is casting it is some distance away. To find the fish itself, draw a mental line through the water, from the shadow towards the sun. The trout you are seeking, will lie some distance from the bottom, somewhere along that line (Fig. 5).

Do not expect a fish such as we have just described to be easy to see. Fish that lie in midwater can be very difficult to see. Indeed, perhaps the most difficult fish of all to see, is one that rides close to the surface, over a gravelled bottom, in briskly flowing, eddying water.

It is one that BC has come to term the "see-through" fish; and which JG refers to with equal validity, as "the shimmer". It is a midwater fish that is characterized by the subtleties of light which play upon it; and not, as in the case of our previous friend, by the light it cuts off the bottom.

The "see-through" fish (Fig. 6) is at his most transparent, on sunny days. The sunlight melts as it passes through the rumpling, rippling surface, and splashes fluidly down his sleek and mobile form; it reflects off the brilliance of his scales, oils down his back, drips off his fins. It dissolves him utterly; and he evaporates into the light, the water and the stones around him.

When you have come to see the see-through fish, you will be seeing most of the trout in the river.

There are two kinds of *line* that betray the trout, as well. The first is on the tail that we have already mentioned: the vertical trailing edge (Fig. 7). It is the most common betrayer of the trout which lies with his head under a weedbed. Presumably he feels safe once the darkness of the fronds closes about his eyes; but like the ostrich that buries his head in the sand he leaves, as it were, something behind. It is surprising how many trout leave their tails protruding: and it is the vertical edge which gives them away, contrasting sharply with the horizontal wafting of the weed alongside.

The other kind of line that should be framed in your mental gallery is the thin, straight line that runs due upstream/downstream. This line is at its most noticeable (and when that is said, it is not saying much) on clear gravel reaches which have few distinguishing features.

It is most easily seen from broadside-on; and for this and other reasons it pays not simply to fix the eyes on the water ahead but on the water opposite, too.

The straight line that runs upstream/downstream is often a trout: a fish whose darker back can just be seen, but whose sides reflect the light and riverbed, and all but disappear.

Fig. 6 The see-through fish: a trout that rides high in rippled water on sunny days, can almost evaporate before the eyes.

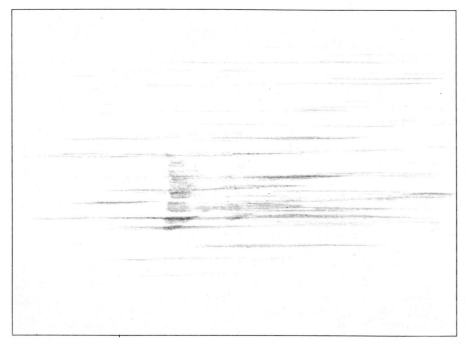

Fig. 7 The underwater world of the river is almost entirely composed of longitudinal lines created by the action of the water, and any weed present. In it, the trailing edge of the trout's tail—which shows up as a vertical thin dark line—can be a revealing clue.

Getting down to the job—JG casts to a nymphing fish

3 Where trout lie

However big he is, and whatever kind of water he inhabits, the trout is an expert at survival: in knowing where the food is, and getting it; and in conserving his energies and keeping out of trouble, when he is not.

But places good for eating in, and places good for surviving in, are by no means necessarily the same: a fact that the fish himself learns at a very early age, if he is to learn at all. As a consequence, it is not possible to say that a fish has "his lie" and so to suggest that the trout has one spot and only one spot, where we can expect to find him on a river.

Some trout *do* have only one lie (see below), but many more have two, three or several at any one time – and, over the course of a year, perhaps a dozen or more, as they accommodate themselves to changes in water levels, the appearance and disappearance of obstacles and features on the riverbed, and to the availability and otherwise of different forms of insect food as the season progresses. For this reason it similarly is not sensible to assume that a fish has been caught because it is not where we have seen it on occasions before. It may have "gone", but it may not have gone permanently or even very far.

Because, as anglers, we are concerned with *feeding* fish, let us consider the needs of the feeding trout, in modest detail. Only by understanding something of his needs will we come to understand (and to exploit) his behaviour.

The principal need of the trout that wants to eat, is food. Much of the food which the trout eats on rivers (although by no means all of it) appears all at once, as it were: typically as in migrations of nymphs and hatches of fly. And it is the sudden appearance of substantial amounts of food, that is the probable trigger of his general feeding response.

The trout soon discovers that tiny, vulnerable creatures like flies and nymphs are at the mercies of the currents, and tend to get concentrated into channels created by the water and its reaction to obstacles to its progress: to impediments like weeds, and stones, and piling and bridge supports. And not unnaturally, the trout positions himself to take advantage of the most concentrated flows (Fig. 8).

These concentrations do not, of course, occur only at the surface. It is perfectly possible for the surface current to be taking floating flies in one direction while a local sub-surface current, created by the reaction of a small area of water to some sub-surface obstacle, takes nymphs in a different direction.

This is a typical circumstance when a single trout may have two or three feeding locations, at any one time of the year – quite apart from the "survival" or "resting" lie which provides him with the security he needs while staying out of trouble, and conserving his strength. One position may be favoured when the food is on, in or immediately beneath the surface film; a second position may be preferred when it is necessary to lie close to the bottom, to acquire what food is on offer. A typical third position would not be a fixed point at all, but a whole area or beat of the water which the trout will patrol when actively hunting food from the riverbed: food like shrimps and caddis larvae, which the current may not naturally bring to his palate.

Fig. 8 A wonderful lie for trout: a narrow channel where the river is forced between the bank on the left and the island in the middle. All the food that the river carries is funnelled down this narrow neck, and the trout queue up one behind the other, in wait for it.

Once he has found a lie, he will prove tenacious and difficult to shift. He will leave if he is driven away by an angler or a bigger fish; or sometimes if a pike takes up residence nearby. But otherwise – at least if he is a brown trout – he will stay. He will display real aggression to other trout that encroach upon his territory, and even if driven away by predators will return as quickly as he can, when the danger has passed.

It is by no means the case that because their basic needs are the same, the trout feeding in the faster and shallower reach leads a similar existence to that of his friend in the slower beat, elsewhere. The two, in their different kinds of lies, lead very different lives.

In fast water, the current brings food down to the trout at a hasty rate: there is a vague shape ahead of him in the stream one moment, it is beside him the next, and being whirled away the second after that. If he is to eat whatever it is that approaches, his decision must be made quickly, and executed just as fast. There is no time for "Oh-dear-me", and "Shall-I-or-shan't-I?" It's now or never, grab or not. So the trout in fast water is a vulnerable trout, for that reason alone: if he grabs, and grabs the wrong fly, he's done for.

But that is not all.

As we shall see in greater detail where we deal with vision, the trout's view of the outside world is not only not very wide (because in shallow water he is by definition nearer the surface, and so has a smaller window): it is often desperately distorted, too.

Water that rushes over the riverbed cannot dictate its course. It must follow the contour of the bed: a bed gouged and riddled, humped and gnarled. Each distortion of the bottom contorts the water flowing over it, creating whorls and vortices, whirlpools and wrinkles, that pucker and pleat the surface film. And it is through all of this that the trout must see, and hope to discern the true from the false.

The trout that lies in fast, shallow water to feed is a mettlesome fish indeed. But he leads a dangerous existence, and not always a long one. Few big fish indeed reside in the shallows, before the urge to mate takes its hold.

The trout that feeds in slower and deeper water leads a very different life. There is no darting this way and that for him; no extrovert and suicidal lunge.

He hangs around midwater; perhaps a little above, perhaps a little below. He can see above, below, to the sides and ahead. His food – unless he lifts some larvae from the bottom, or rummages for shrimps amid the weed – arrives in conspicuous and stately procession.

He can see it approaching from a long way off: and not in single, tiny morsels that must be concentrated upon intently lest some fluke of the current sweeps them away, but in tens and dozens and hundreds from which he can take his pick.

The trout in slower, deeper water is a choosy trout when he wants to be: he has all the time in the world to scrutinize, if he cares to take it – and quite often he does.

Lies – specific

As we have indicated elsewhere, exactly which lie the trout chooses on a particular day will be influenced by many factors: by his size, and the range of options physically open to him; by the time of year; by the height of the water; by the direction and strength of the wind; and by many other factors including, not least, the kind of food his beat supports.

Few lies are satisfactory in all conditions, providing not only food when it is wanted, but security (which means an amenable current, and protection from predators) when it isn't; and those that are, are contested vigorously by the fish.

Fig. 9 The outside of a bend is a classical place for a trout to lie. On this slow, wide reach looking upstream, the bend is the only feature to influence the current: the current comes gently into the bank on the left and condenses more food there than it does elsewhere. On bends like this, most fish will be found within two or three yards of the bank. Just as we took this picture a trout decided to reinforce our observation, by rising.

That, of course, is the reason why lies that are obviously "good" as defined above *hold* big fish, and often aggressive fish: fish, in other words, that are capable of fighting off incursions by their lesser brethren.

In the list of typical lies and holding places which follows, only two or three fall into the year-round category. In *every* case, however, where the lie is a feeding lie, there will by definition be a supply of food: and almost always a narrower band of current, a channel or an eddy to concentrate it further.

When looking for likely lies on any stretch of any river, look in the first instance for concentrations in the principal line of the current (for example, where the weight of water pushes into the *outside* of the bend – Fig. 9); and in the second instance, look for eddies *off* the principal current.

And so to specific lies.

Bridges

Any fisherman with more than a morning's experience knows that the water beneath a bridge is a likely lie for a trout; and often, for a big trout (Fig. 10). It is that rare phenomenon, the "complete" lie.

It is not difficult to see why. A bridge is usually sited on the narrowest section of river compatible with its main purpose. And the narrower a section of the river is, the deeper it will be: in the absence of Moses, the water cannot rise up; it must dip down by carving away the bottom. So the water beneath the average bridge tends to be deeper than the norm; and if the bridge has arches, the bottom becomes more deeply sculpted still, where the current is deflected from the sides and supports.

As a result, all the food borne by the river is not simply channelled into a narrow thrust of water where the banks close in: it is deflected into secondary, and even tighter channels.

If you can see under the arch of the bridge, look first at the point, some way below the upstream side, at which the thrusts of current shrugged off by the structures converge.

Most of the river's drifting food will be funnelled into that point, and the trout will be waiting there, with jaws agape. If no fish is apparent there – look then along the *sides* of the bridge, whence the food will have been carried by the back-eddy.

(Bridges, marvellous constructions though they often are, have two disadvantages that every angler knows. There are unwritten laws – indeed, so consistently do they manifest themselves that they probably *are* written; and enshrined, it may further be surmised, in finest copperplate – about bridges and the fish which lie beneath them. The first is that the lower the bridge is and the more difficult it is to cast beneath, the larger any trout will be. If it is utterly impossible to cast beneath a bridge, then there a grand-daddy will lie. The second law states that a wind will blow in any direction *other* than upstream, under a bridge!)

Fig. 10 A low bridge with a deep wide pool scoured out beneath it is one of the most classical of all trout lies. A very big fish lives under this bridge. He's been there for years!

Hatch pools

If there is one place on the river where a big fish will be found – a place even more likely than a very low bridge to be attractive to the grand-daddy of the stream – then it is the hatch pool.

Because of the immense weight of water pouring down on it from the gate above, the hatch pool is always an area of deep water; water, sometimes, to be measured in the tens of feet. And because of the fall, it is well-oxygenated, even in the hottest weather.

Look, first, for any sandbanks or gravel banks that might have been built up from the bed. Pay particular atttention to the head of such a bank, and to the sides.

Expect the fish, too, to lie in the eddies (of course!) just off the main current; and (of course!) tight into the banks where the current bites.

Look, too, towards the tail of the pool, where the floor begins to shelve up and the water becomes a glassy glide: fish will often fall back to such a position in the evening; and in the daytime too, if there is a heavy hatch of fly.

Look *on top of the hatch*. It is common for a fish to lie immediately in front of the lip, where the torrent pours down into the pool below, apparently holding station by miraculous powers; almost immobile save for a gentle drift of an inch or two, to either side.

In fact, of course, no fish could live in the full force of the current that forges through the hatch itself and the trout, very sensibly, lies a fraction below the lip where the current is all but negligible; or hangs poised on the cushion of current that pushes back upstream, where the water bounces off the hatch support.

The position at the top of the hatch is a marvellous lie for a fish. But be warned on two counts. He will usually be a nervous, wary fish, that will be difficult to approach; and if you hook him, he'll like as not turn downstream, over the fall and into the pool below.

(Such a trout can be fun. JG remembers a particularly sophisticated and frustrating fish. The trout lay on top of a hatch for several years, and grew big and wise. The pool below his hatch was – unusually – safe for bathing in; and so was much used by local youths for that unreasonable pursuit. To get to the pool, a footbridge across the top of the hatch had to be used. As a consequence, the fish grew very accustomed to human traffic, and its significance. A man who crossed the bridge immediately behind the trout with a towel under his arm, prompted not a flicker of interest. A man who danced upon the footbridge and waved his arms like a windmill in order to frighten the fish, would have collapsed with exhaustion without succeeding. But whenever, year upon year, JG poked the end of a rod stealthily over the bankside to attempt something unspeakable, the trout departed amid an indignant cloud of silt!)

Fig. 11 A weir, sill or waterfall is a near-certain place to find trout. The fish lie in depressions on the bottom, in the last yard or so of water before it tumbles over the edge. Two fish are lying on the sill in this photograph.

Sills and weirs

All that has been said about the fish lying on top of the hatchpool applies to the trout that lies on the top of a sill or weir (Fig. 11), with the qualification that the river is not always narrow at such a point, and so the flow of food is less concentrated.

It is by no means uncommon to find a line of fish in position in the glassy water at the immediate upstream edge of the fall.

Because the food is no more concentrated there than it is in the body of the river, it is our belief that such fish have taken up positions there for reasons of physical comfort: because the current, the temperature and the oxygen content of the water itself are more agreeable to the fish that have assumed them than they are in the other lies available to those fish, at that time, elsewhere.

Overhanging trees

Trees that grow up from the water's edge provide for many of the needs of trout, simply by being there. For example, they provide him with physical cover, which helps to protect him from predators, from the direct heat of the sun, from the full glare of the light. And, of course, they are the scene of much insect activity and life, so providing the occasional supplementary meal. So any tree which hangs over the river, starts off with a plus.

But there are some trees that mark the lies of fish with all the certainty of a finger from the clouds (though you're unlikely to see that, polaroids or no). These are the trees that hang over deeper pools at the ends of shallows, and under which the current cuts.

If one adds to such golden embellishments a breeze that pushes floating flies into the bank beneath the tree, then there's a good chance that any fish there will be a rising fish.

In circumstances such as these (and, when they occur, under tussocks of grass that grow up from the edge of the bank) do not look for your fish in the general direction of the overhanging fronds: the fish, if the current and the wind penetrate that far, will lie so close to the bank as almost to touch it. A foot or 18 inches out can be too far.

Rocks and other impediments

Almost every book we have read has drawn attention to the importance of rocks, logs and the like on the riverbed, which act as impediments to the progress of the water. And almost without fail, these books have urged the reader to concentrate his attentions on the downstream side of such obstacles, "where the trout lie in wait for the food".

This is one of those pieces of advice that while sometimes helpful, more often is not.

It is perfectly true that trout often lie in wait for food on the inside edges of eddies which such obstacles often create, on their downstream sides.

But far more often – except in very fast water – the trout lie *in front* of rocks, and to the sides of them. And the man who has concentrated his attention *behind* such things has been missing at least half of the fish on offer. And if, hitherto, he has been a wet-fly man fishing down and across, carefully allowing his flies to swing behind the obstacle from his upstream position, he has been lining a high proportion of fish in the river.

The trout likes the upstream sides of rocks, logs, and goodness-knows-not-what other solid objects that may from time to time appear, for exactly the same reasons that he likes the tops of hatches: because he has a splendid view of what the current is bringing him; and yet is cushioned from the weight of the water.

(But note that there is one exception to all of this. The American cutthroat trout prefers to lie *downstream* of obstacles, almost regardless of the pace of the water. Though with a name like that, he can be forgiven for almost any aberration.)

Weedbeds

A useful rule of thumb for the man wanting to find the trout in his river would be, "where there is weed, there are fish" (Fig. 12).

Weed provides the trout with cover. It harbours the food that he needs in order to live – often in dense concentrations. And, of course, it provides him with places to lie: in the calmer water at the head of the weedbed, where the roots form an obstruction to the flow; and beneath it and downstream of it where the constant sweeping to and fro has eroded channels and dips in the bed.

Look, also, at the top of two distinct weedbeds that emerge side-by-side from the bottom. The current that each root-hold shrugs off must find a way between them: and so must the food that the current carries. The trout knows it, just as surely as he knows it under bridges, where the same thing occurs.

Pockets and channels

The trout will take up a position that the inexperienced angler will dismiss at a glance. Often, such a position will occur on broad and apparently featureless shallows.

Fig. 12 A healthy current, weed and a pocket of deep water. Wherever these three come together, expect to find a fish. When BC took this photograph his hands were still wet from a wild, 2 lb brown trout he had just removed from the scoop beneath the weedbed.

We all know shallows like this. They occur below rapids, and below the glides where deep pools run off. The river is unusually wide. When the sun is behind the back or overhead, every pebble, every fish, every *caddis*, can be taken in at a glance. It is patently clear that there is nothing there.

Or is there? The real answer is "yes – trout". The reason why they are there is because we got the premise wrong. The bottom is not featureless. It has small pockets in it, in which trout lie. It has channels in the river bed, up which trout patrol. Not deep pockets, or deep channels; simply depressions. Where, typically, the average depth across the flats is a foot or so, the depression may be 18 inches; where the average depth is six inches, a channel may be a foot deep.

Such features are very difficult to see. The experienced observer of fish will see the trout before he sees the pocket or channel. Sometimes they will only be discovered by accident, while wading. It is a rare flat that possesses no features at all.

Silt on the current

There are two valuable clues to lies that are provided by silt suspended on the current.

The most common cause of silt on the current is a fish that you will not catch. Not yet, that is. This fish lies well down, close to the bottom. He has a splendid view through his big, wide window; and an excellent chance of seeing you, before you see him.

When he *does* see you, he departs. The powerful thrust of his body sends up a cloud of silt from the bottom, that quickly attracts the eye (Fig. 13).

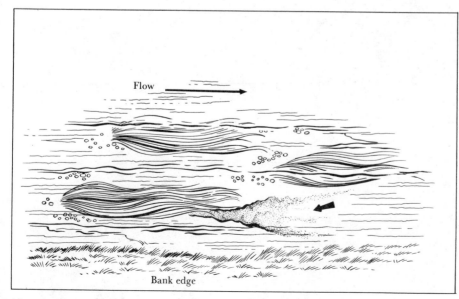

Fig. 13 Among the minor but important clues the observant angler will recognise, is a puff of silt drifting down on the current. Sometimes it will have been created by a fish that has seen him, and bolted; sometimes it will betray a fish lying some way upstream that is rummaging among the weeds, for nymphs.

Flow

Bank edge

In the case of this fish, simply make an accurate mental note of his position, and move on. Next time you're on his territory you'll approach more cautiously, and know exactly where to look.

The other clue that silt can provide can be capitalized upon, at once. It manifests itself merely as a slight greying of the water, in a narrow stream, in an otherwise crystalline river.

It is a forewarning and not, this time, a sign that your fish has gone.

Thin, constant streams of silt on the current are often caused by fish some distance upstream, rummaging among the weeds for nymphs; or fish that are (see "Clues to Feeding Behaviour") twisting onto their sides to pick shrimps from tight on the bottom.

Whenever such a clue is seen it is a signal to move cautiously, to look hard, and to reach for your weighted patterns.

Big-game hunters at work: JG and BC trapping nymphs for study

4 The light patch

There is one phenomenon concerning the lies of fish in some rivers that is of such great importance that we feel we should address it separately.

It is a subject upon which, at the time of writing, neither of us has seen anything written, anywhere: and yet it provides an instantaneous key to the location of large numbers of trout, in those waters on which the phenomenon occurs.

It has, we believe, a revolutionary significance not only in the pursuit of trout, but in the hunting of other territorial fish, too; and not just on alkaline rivers, but on any river in which there occurs mild algal growth on the bottom; trace growths of filamentous weeds on the bottom; or mild depositions of silt on slow reaches, or on other reaches in periods of low water or drought.

Fig. 14 A sure give-away of trout lies on river bottoms where algae bloom: light patches, worn away by the tails of fish, give the impression of a pale rash on these broad shallows.

We have termed this phenomenon, with stunning lack of imagination, "the light patch".

The light patch is simply a small area of the river bed that is marginally lighter in colour than the riverbed around (Figs. 14 and 15). It is caused by a fish of some size holding its position in the current, tight on the bottom: and by the continuous wafting from side to side of his tail.

As the tail pulses softly in the current twice or thrice each second, for hours, days and weeks, the tiny turbulence it creates and the fish's occasional physical contact with the bottom, brushes off any slight deposit or growth of vegetable matter, and simply cleans the stones and bottom beneath. On some chalk streams the exposed bed, cleaned of debris, can gleam like a heliograph. It is a circumstance which we have witnessed on countless occasions; and when we have removed a trout from a particularly well-marked spot, the lower edge of his tail fin has occasionally shown signs of considerable wear (Fig. 16).

In documenting this phenomenon, it should not be taken that we are implying that *all* light patches on the bottom of a trout stream are caused by the fish themselves. Clearly, that would be nonsense. Many light patches are caused by freakish turbulence in the current, where it curls behind stones and the like. But sufficient numbers *are* caused by fish, to justify closer scrutiny of all light patches on the river bed than is accorded to any of the more obvious potential lies that we have discussed so far.

Nor, it should be noted, are we suggesting that all fish are capable of leaving their marks in this way, when they lie for a period of time, on the bottom. Very small fish are not, in our experience, capable of creating sufficient turbulence (though, certainly, a *shoal* of small coarse fish is).

Nor are we suggesting that every river provides the conditions in which even a large fish will leave his mark: in particular, the clean-scoured bottom of the upland spate river – even one artificially stocked with larger fish – would not do so. But many rivers already do; and as pollution spreads, and algal growths spread with it, more may yet do so.

Fig. 15 A light patch in close-up. In this case the small shingle of the bottom has been physically displaced by the vigorous sweep of a big trout's tail. (See separate picture in colour section.)

Where conditions are ideal – and we have observed light patches caused by fish on many rivers – the change of colour denoted by a single patch can often be sufficiently dramatic to be visible fifty yards away. *Fifty yards away.* Imagine being able to pinpoint a fish on the bottom, within inches, at such a great distance. As a marker, it is more valuable even than a rise-form, because the rise-form drifts back with the current, and the light patch does not.

Consider, if you will, how many times *you* have observed "patches of gravel" on a stony bottom, or "patches of sand" on a gravel bottom; or places where the chalk "has come right to the surface". Consider how many times you can recall seeing fish in such places, or near them. There was no coincidence about that proximity: the fish were showing you where they lived.

So common are light patches, in rivers or areas of rivers that have light algal or weed growth on the bottom, or filmy deposits of silt, that broad shallows can look as though they have been waded across in studded boots, by a stumbling giant (Fig. 14 again).

Fig. 16 Three stages of tail-wear caused by constant contact with the bottom. In Fig. 16A the wear is very pronounced, while in 16B it is less pronounced but still quite noticeable. In Fig. 16C the wear is almost imperceptible—but nevertheless visible when one knows where to look: note that the upper edge of this fish's tail is sleekly convex while the lower edge has been worn flat. Note also the startling differences in the shapes of these three tails, all belonging to wild fish taken from the same reach of the same river. The wearing and thickening of the lower edge of the tail through contact with the bottom is not confined to the trout. We have noticed similar wear on the tails of some big grayling.

But the light patch is invaluable in looking for trout in deep water, too. It glows from the bottom like a beacon in the night. Not with that intensity, of course, but with that significance, once its possible causes have been understood.

Even if you do not see a trout on a light patch (and, because he may have several lies, you may well not) do not be in too much of a hurry to move on. He *may*, of course, have been caught. But it is every bit as common for a trout to lie a foot upstream of the light patch, as it is for him to lie directly upon it.

If a fish is not immediately apparent, look for the fanning of his tail at the upstream edge of the patch. It is his tail that causes most of the erosion, as explained a moment ago: and most erosion occurs just behind him, because that is where the current carries the turbulence he creates.

(Note, too, that in very shallow water, an unoccupied light patch may well mark an evening lie. Shallow-water lies are often only occupied by fish under the cover of darkness – in part, no doubt, because the trout feels less vulnerable then.)

Communal lies

Discovery of the significance of the light patch has led us to observe another interesting phenomenon: the communal lie or boundary post. We normally term it the former, though it may well be the latter.

The "communal lie" is a large light area on the bottom of the river, that is intermittently crossed by several fish: sometimes singly, sometimes – briefly – by two or even three fish at a time. We have seen the communal lie on several occasions; and in each case the large areas of lighter coloration have clearly been caused not by the action of any one fish, but by the actions of several fish continually crossing and recrossing a fixed point on the riverbed.

With the whole of the river available it is something of a mystery why the fish should, time after time, cross a given point – usually located, we have found, at the extreme downstream ends of their individual beats.

The fish appear on the light patch they have created, linger for a moment or two, and then move on. When more than one fish arrives on the patch at the same time, the individuals show no territorial aggression, but sheer gently off, onto their individual beats.

It has been clear to us that the communal lie is not a feeding or survival lie in the sense that we have discussed them so far: but equally clearly they are points in the water which are shared – if momentarily – by several fish with beats of their own.

The most probable explanation is that the "communal lie" is a common boundary point that marks the limits to the beat of each fish.

However it comes to be created, the communal lie is an interesting phenomenon. But for practical angling significance, the "light patch" leaves it standing. The light patch is of profound importance to the angler.

5 Clues to feeding behaviour

The Achilles Heel of the trout lies – if we may be permitted a particularly stiff metaphorical cocktail – in his stomach: in the fact that he must eat to live, and becomes vulnerable the moment he opens his mouth to satisfy himself.

There is, of course, no absolute certainty that because a trout has opened his mouth to take our fly, then he has taken it in mistake for the kind of food he is used to eating (or, for that matter, that he has taken it in mistake for any kind of food at all).

The only utter certainty about a fish that we bring to the net on a fly, is that it has taken the fly into its mouth *because that is where the fly clearly is when we see it.* Any question of how it came to be there – what motivated the fish to take the fly into its mouth in the first place – will forever remain hypothesis, unless a fish can be persuaded to talk.

But when that is said, there *are* grounds for assuming that when a fish feeding selectively upon, say, small flies of a particular kind takes a small artificial dressed to imitate such creatures, then that fish has taken the artificial in mistake for the real thing. G.E.M. Skues said he would give up the game if he believed anything else; and a long march of anglers would wind the road behind him, if they did not believe the same. It is the fundamental premise upon which all imitative fly-fishing on rivers is based; and it is a premise which all of us accept.*

So the challenge for the fly-fisherman becomes – how can we exploit this gastronomic chink in the trout's scaly armour: the chink that makes him open his mouth to eat, and that makes him vulnerable the moment he does so?

Far and away the greatest step any angler can take towards capturing the trout is to acquire an understanding of its feeding behaviour; and in particular, of the relationship between the behaviour of the trout and the kind of insect it wishes to eat.

It is one of the most important things to understand in the whole of fly-fishing, that the feeding movements of the trout are not random, and without consequence. Trout move in characteristic ways, when pursuing creatures of different species which are themselves moving in different ways, in and upon the water; and these movements, and the water displacements which result from them when the fish are feeding at or near the surface, can be interpreted to provide golden clues for the fly-fisher.

Let us look at them together, now.

*This is not to say that we believe all trout take feathered confections on hooks, in the belief that such confections are food. Very often we believe, lake trout take lures and streamers out of curiosity and/or aggression. The reader wishing to find a detailed analysis of the possible motivations of trout attaching themselves to lures in lakes will find it in Brian Clarke's book *The Pursuit of Stillwater Trout* (A. & C. Black, 1975).

THE RISE AS A GUIDE TO THE FLY

The principle of interpretation

Elsewhere we have observed that the trout, like all other creatures in the wild, is concerned to save energy.

His desire to do this is not, of course, the product of a thinking process, any more than anything else a trout does is the product of a thinking process. The desire exists simply because that is the way that evolution, and the laws of survival, have chosen to make it.

Given that the trout is concerned not to expend energy uselessly, it is a reasonable assumption that in the main, he will not expend more energy in pursuit of an item of food than he will replace by consuming it.

It will, of course, happen from time to time, and on occasion several fish will be seen to do the same – for example, when there is competition for the sudden appearance of a limited amount of a particularly desirable food. But commonsense dictates that our premise must by and large be sound, or else the trout would long since have ceased to exist. His ancestors would have grown weaker and weaker; and no creature in the wild needs to ask twice what happens when that deadly descent is begun.

So as a general consequence of our premise, we can reasonably say that if a creature which the trout wants to eat is moving only slowly, then the trout will itself move only slowly, to catch and eat it. And commonsense similarly dictates that if a creature which a trout wants to eat is moving at high speed, then the trout itself will simply *have* to move at high speed, if it is to overhaul its prey, and dine.

So the first point that it is necessary to store away in understanding the principle of rise-forms, is that in general trout move slowly when eating slowly moving creatures, and briskly when eating swiftly moving creatures.

In other words, that there is a direct relationship between the speed of the trout, and the locomotive capacities of the insect it wishes to eat.

Now let us look at the water in which the "rise-form" is revealed, and see what we can deduce from that.

A trout swims – for the sake of simplicity – by thrusting its body from side to side. Each time it thrusts, it displaces the water alongside its flanks. If it swims quickly, it will be thrusting vigorously, and so will displace water with some violence. If it swims slowly, then the more leisurely movements of its body will displace water more gently.

But wait! Does this not mean that there is not only a relationship between the speed of the trout and the speed of the creature it is pursuing, but a relationship, too, between the speed of the trout, and the violence with which the water is displaced?

Yes, indeed.

And does this not now complete the linkage? Do we not now have a link between the movement (or absence of movement) on the part of the wee creature at the start of it all, and the water displacement (or "rise-form") that we see?

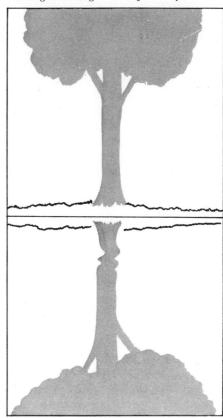

Indeed, dear Watson, it does, and we do. It means that by using our wits and powers of observation, we can look at many kinds of rise and have an excellent idea of the kinds of creature that might have prompted them, simply by knowing what kinds of creatures move in which kinds of ways, and where.

The discovery of the principles behind movement and rise-forms, is about as close to the Philosopher's Stone that the fly-fisherman is likely (or, indeed, would want) to get. With the mental reference points which they provide, let us look now at the rise-forms that can be regularly observed; and let us see what they can tell us about the gastronomic preferences of the fish that cause them.

And let us do something else, as well. Let us see what we can discover from the trout that feeds *below* the surface, regardless of whether or not he can be seen directly, and whether or not he creates a "rise-form". Not all fish, even in clear-water, alkaline streams, can be seen all of the time – but that does not mean they are not there. Sometimes it is because they are concealed by reflected light. Sometimes it is because they are concealed by surface ripple. Sometimes it is because they lie deep down in hidden places that are fruitful to them but impenetrable to us.

Indeed, let us look at these most coy among our fishy friends, first. Often – though deliciously unaware of the fact – they reveal where they are, and what they're up to, to the man who is prepared to use his eyes, and to engage his brain behind them.

LOCATING INVISIBLE FISH

A – Reflections

One of the most common – and the most subtle – of all the ways in which an unseen fish can betray its presence, is by causing a small movement in the otherwise still reflections in the surface film on smooth water.

As we discussed in a previous chapter, there are reflections in the surface of all smooth stretches of river, when the sun is not behind or overhead: reflections of the opposite bank, of trees and buildings; of distant features of the terrain, like hills.

They do not always stay constant in *tone*, because of changes in the intensity of the light; but all reflections will have a constancy of shape and sharpness that is "right" for the reach and conditions at the time. Right, that is, until a fish swims beneath the surface with sufficient violence to shift them.

Then, the reflection of a hitherto straight tree trunk might suddenly acquire a curve, or an S-bend (Fig. 17). The outline of a building might blur for a moment or two, at just one point. In an area of dark reflections as we discussed in the matter of seeing fish, small winks of light might suddenly appear. In an area of light, localized patches of dark may briefly be observed. All these clues – and others besides – are excellent indications of a fish: and a moving (and so possibly feeding) fish at that. It is the man who observes such subtle clues who has a flying start over the man who does not. Simply knowing

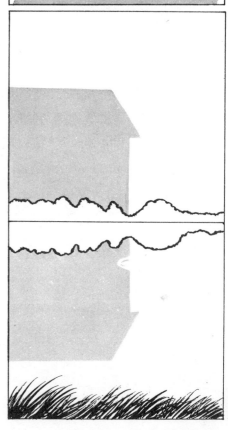

that a fish is there prompts him to find a position from which the fish itself might become visible. If such a position cannot be attained, a well-placed throw will often bring him a response, nonetheless.

It is, of course, such an occasional, apparently random throw which consistently delivers fish, that gives men reputations for "sixth senses"; or some mysterious communion with the wild. It is nothing of the sort. The "random" throw to the spectator who has missed the clues might merely be the *coup de grâce* of the man behind the rod.

B – The cross-current ripple

The water does not have to be silken smooth to reveal the presence of fish which cannot be seen from the bankside. As we mentioned briefly when discussing what the observant angler might expect to see in the water, one of the most common indications of all occurs in rolling, eddying, fast-flowing water.

Eddies and ripples in a river might to a non-fisherman look simply like a confusion of undulations and swirls. But even the tyro fisherman soon comes to see that they are not: that there is a pattern or rhythm to events with, as we observed, always the preponderance of movement occurring in a downstream direction.

While all eddies and ripples are different, observation for only a few moments will show what is characteristic of them, on a given piece of water. The clues begin to come, when anything uncharacteristic is thereafter observed.

The most common clue occurs when a tress of downstream ripples is momentarily interrupted at some point in its course by a procession of ripples *across the general flow* (Fig. 18).

Fig. 18 A subtle indication of a trout's presence in broken water, is created by a fish as it turns sharply to intercept an item of food below the surface. The water pushed upwards by the trout's flank reaches the surface, and causes a momentary break in the pattern of ripples created by the downstream flow of the current.

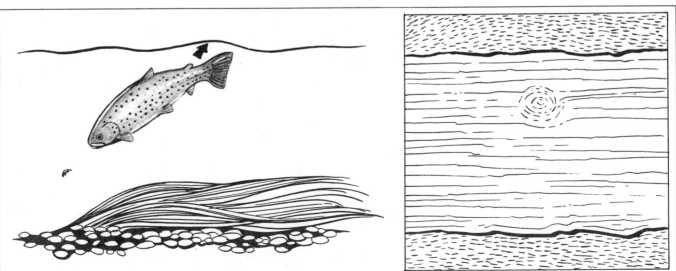

Such a widthways disturbance does not last long – it will be gone in a second or two – but it has almost certainly been caused by a fish whirling to take something below the surface: its sudden lunge has sent an upthrust of water heaving to the top. The "boil" reaches the surface partly dissipated by the force of the current, but holds up long enough to break or disturb the existing rumples. The result is a series of cross-current ripples.

Such a phenomenon is unmistakable to the man who knows what he is looking for, and all but invisible to the man who does not.

All of the above concerns, of course, an upthrust of water caused by a fish pursuing a nymph in broken water. On slow or smooth water the water will actually appear to bulge when a fish takes a nymph close to the surface.

C – The sub-surface "rise"

The sub-surface rise is a "rise-form" that causes more confusion, and more exploration of the Anglo-Saxon vocabulary, than any other.

The problem arises because, in calm water, the disturbance created by a fish taking a nymph, pupa, or shrimp close to the surface, or one of those species of spinners that drifts along just beneath the film, can easily be mistaken for a rise to surface fly.

The inability to distinguish between the "rise" to the emerging nymph and the rise to the surface fly proper, is perhaps the single most common cause of failure, when the fish respond to a hatch. Alas, there is no short cut. The only way the two can consistently be told apart is by practised observation. The answer is to look long and hard, before deciding what to offer. And the first step in that process is to watch the fate of any surface flies that you can see drifting over the position of the fish. If these flies are taken, then you have your answer. If they are not taken, or if no surface fly is in evidence, then you've *probably* got your answer and it will be the converse. (Fish, as we shall soon see, are quite capable of taking flies from the surface that are wholly invisible from five yards away.)

The reason that distinction between the surface and sub-surface fly is so important is that a trout preoccupied with sub-surface food is unlikely to rise to surface artificials, no matter how perfectly tied and delicately delivered. The reverse, however, is not the case. The trout that is feeding at the surface is quite often prepared to settle for a nymph, for reasons best understood by itself.

D – The "twist"

The interpretation of specific kinds of feeding behaviour in fish, is one of the highest levels of sophistication to which the fly-fisherman can aspire. It is also one of the most rewarding, in terms of understanding the fish in its environment; and *the* most important, as a means of adding trout to the bag.

The "twist" is a common feeding movement below the water surface, and

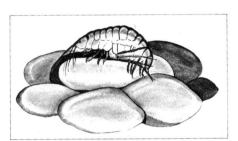

Fig. 19 Shrimps clinging to stones on the bottom prompt trout to move in an unusual way to dislodge them. (See the colour photograph on page 81.)

interpretation of it embodies each of the satisfactions outlined above.

The "twist" (see colour photograph on page 81) is a semi-corkscrewing action in which the trout – which invariably is lying close to the bottom – rolls on its side for a second or so at a very acute angle to the riverbed, and then resumes its normal, dorsal-up position. It is a movement that can be repeated over and over again, and reveals the predilection of a fish for shrimps.

The shrimp (Fig. 19) is a furtive creature that lives, when there is no weed about, hard down among the stones on the bottom; clinging onto them hunchbacked, head down, with all his tiny legs. He has a marked lack of enthusiasm for his wider role in the chain of life; and goes out of his way, indeed, to avoid it. When he needs to move, he moves around the sides of stones; and under the arches formed where stones abut; and he clambers down cracks and wrinkles in their surface if traverse them he must, to avoid the attentions of the trout. So on stony reaches, the trout rarely has the chance to nab a shrimp in midwater. If he wants a shrimp, he must pick one off the bottom with his mouth.

It is primarily for this reason, we believe, that the trout engages himself in the "twist" on stony ground. He engages in it because he must; because his mouth is the wrong shape for picking a moving, reluctant creature off the surface of a stone.

If the trout wants a shrimp that is crawling along the bottom, *he must roll onto his side, and shovel it off with the flat side of his mouth.*

An occasional secondary purpose of the "twist" may be to flush shrimps from the bottom, so that the trout can take them midwater. But we believe this purpose to *be* secondary because only infrequently is a fish seen to make the characteristic dart and snap at midwater food, once the body-twist has been completed. The "twist", almost always, is a self-contained action.

The "tailing" trout

"Tailing" is a feeding activity which bridges the gap – literally as well as metaphorically – between fish feeding below the surface, and fish feeding *at* the surface; an activity which often sees the tail of the fish waving cheerfully in the air while it is busy removing goodies from weedbeds and the bottom, in very shallow water. It is a "rise-form" that – even for the sophisticated fisherman – can pose problems of distinction, unless it is observed from close quarters (Fig. 20).

The "tailing" fish is most often feeding upon shrimps, nymphs, aquatic snails and caddis. As its head goes down its tail comes up and breaks the surface film, either continuously or spasmodically.

When the tail is almost continuously above the surface film – by half an inch, an inch or more, the effect is very much like that caused by a single stem of reed which breaks the surface: a fine V of water runs downstream for a short distance before the current thins it out, and causes the disturbance to disappear. It is an easy matter, because of this, to walk by a "tailing" fish that feeds in shallow margins, or in reaches abounding with reeds. When the tail breaks the surface only spasmodically, the effect is very much like a rise to the spent fly or "spinner" that is trapped in the surface film (see below).

The "head-and-tail" rise

The "head-and-tail" rise is the nearest thing to a surface rise that the trout actually makes without, as it were, going all the way. Few sights set the fly-fisherman's adrenalin flowing more swiftly.

The head-and-tail rise always seems to happen in breathless slow motion, frame by cinematic frame: first the top of the head appears; then the shoulders, back and dorsal fin; and finally that big, broad tail.

It seems to be a characteristic of the rise that it flatters the size of the fish which makes it. A head-and-tailing trout always seems to be some kind of sinuous and utterly monstrous submarine; yet when it comes out, it looks extraordinarily like a trout, and extraordinarily like an ordinary trout, at that.

The head-and-tail rise is rarely seen in fast-flowing, broken water or rapids. It is a phenomenon of the smoother reaches; and it is usually to nymphs or spinners that have become trapped below the surface film; and to midge pupae similarly immobilized.

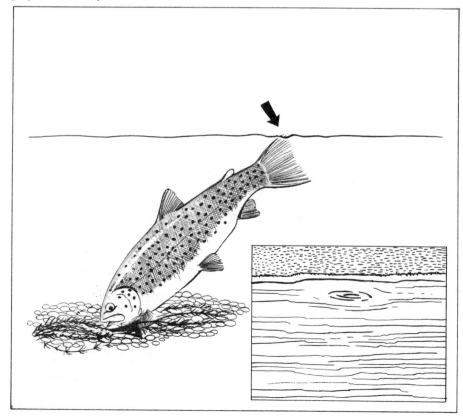

Fig. 20 The "tailing" trout—one which in shallow water leaves his tail behind in the air while his nose is busy grubbing food from the bottom—can create problems of interpretation unless observed at close quarters. The disturbance his tail can leave in the surface film can often appear very like a rise to spent surface fly, when seen from some distance away.

SURFACE RISE-FORMS

The "sip" or "kiss" rise

In our view, though we have chosen to deal with it in its strict position in the sequence of events, the "sip" or "kiss" rise is the most interesting of all the rise-forms that the angler sees. It is also the rise that enables us to demonstrate most comprehensively how careful observation and a little thought can be combined to produce an insight into the world of the fish, and the techniques that might be employed to deceive him. We will examine the rise in detail.

The "sip" or "kiss" rise (Fig. 21) embodies two distinct characteristics. The first is the distinct, audible kissing noise we hear; the second is a small, pinpoint, almost imperceptible disturbance of the surface film – little more than an ebbing full-stop that is swiftly contorted and then dispersed by the current.

In attempting to fathom the secret of the kiss, the first question that needs to be answered is, "Why should a fish taking in food make a kissing noise?" Or put another way, "What must a fish making such a noise be doing?"

And what does commonsense suggest the answer must be? It suggests that a fish making a kissing noise is *not only* sucking in flies. To make that audible sip, it *must* be taking in a little water *and air as well* (try sipping hot soup off a spoon, and see what we mean).

And what does this reveal? It reveals that of all the depths at which fish can feed, the one we are interested in is feeding right at the surface film, *because that is where the air is.*

The second important point that can be deduced is that the trout we are watching is swimming very slowly, if, indeed, it is swimming at all (and the trout, like the seagull on a breeze, does not have to work to move: he can simply adjust his fins, and float up on the current).

Fig. 21 The kiss rise is one of the most fascinating of all rise forms. It has two characteristics: (a) an audible sipping noise created by the brief but powerful suck that the trout uses to bring the fly (and with it some air) down to its position in the water; and (b) the tiniest dimpling disturbance that it creates in the surface film.

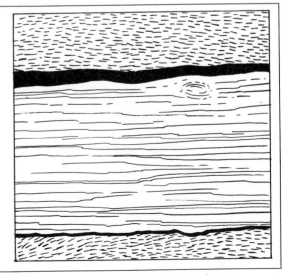

How can we deduce that the fish is not swimming at any kind of speed? Because we know the fish is right at the surface (where the air is) and yet is making only the tiny surface disturbance that we can see: that punctilious, ebbing full-stop. *And would not a fish travelling quickly right at the surface create a commotion, because of the water he would displace?*

Indeed he would. (It is an aside – but one worth making here. The very gentleness of the "sip" rise is often indicative of a large trout that has learned to feed on surface food, while expending the minimum amount of energy. Very large trout rarely make a commotion when feeding.)

There is a third point that can reasonably be deduced from this rise. It is that the fish is absolutely certain that the creature it is after is motionless in the surface film, and cannot get away.

How? Because, attentive dear Watson, of the utterly confident, leisurely and precise way that he sucks in the fly. If the fly had any serious chance of escape – if it had wings up and was capable of making off – instinct and experience would have told an animal that survives by ensuring an adequate return on its output of energy, to hurry things along. Just because the trout has *not* hurried things along, it is a sound assumption it knows it has no need: we have already established that, nine times out of ten, a creature in the wild only moves briskly when it has to.

And so we're almost there. There is only one question left that the fly-fisherman must ask before putting up an appropriate artificial, and casting it with a high degree of confidence. It is: what flies can we expect to find in or on the surface film (where the air is) that cannot get away (because the fish shows no urgency when intercepting them)? And the answer to that, of course, is only flies that are dead or dying, and that are trapped *by* the surface film.

Many flies, of course, find a watery grave; but those which most commonly promote the "sipping" rise are the "spent" spinners that have collapsed onto the water to die, after laying their eggs. Their legs collapse or break through the film, their bodies break into it, and their wings adhere, cruciform, to its treacherous cloy.

After the spent fly, perhaps the most common creature to die at the surface is the hatching nymph.

Not all aquatic flies manage to extricate themselves cleanly from the nymphal shuck. A great many fail to pull their bodies clear; or else they get a wing caught in the nymphal sleeve, or one or more wings stuck, like the spent fly, to the surface. Still others do not give themselves the opportunity to die from natural causes. In their desperate struggles to pull themselves free they send out a thousand tiny, ebbing rings – and so attract attention to themselves. And if there is one thing that the trout seems unable to resist, it is the sight of a struggling fly that cannot get away.

(In heavy hatches of fly, indeed, the trout can be observed to occupy himself not with the plain-sailing dun, but with the dun that flutters about before it becomes airborne. These unfortunates semaphore their presence to the fish, and self-select themselves for eating. Some observations on how the angler might capitalize on this are made in the chapter on dry-fly fishing.)

Yet another kind of insect that gets caught in the surface film, as opposed to the creature which stands *on* the surface film, is the terrestrial fly, beetle or grub which falls onto the water. Such animals are wholly unequipped for the aquatic life; and as they struggle, so they penetrate deeper into the film, and at the same time become weaker and weaker – much, appalling thought that it is, like the man who falls into a marsh.

The effect is very much the same; and the end is usually just as assured.

The "slash"

No rise-form to surface food could be in sharper contrast to the pinpoint delicacy of the "kiss" rise, than the rise we have termed the "slash" (see colour photograph on page 80). Like the kiss rise, however, it can be interpreted with a little thought.

The slash rise is exactly what the term suggests – a powerful, large-scale disturbance of the surface, in which either spray is hurled high into the air, or there is a powerful, lateral surfing of water.

For exactly the reasons that the delicate and pinpoint kiss was made by a slow-moving fish at the surface, so the slash is created by a fast-moving fish at the surface (how else could the water be broken with such violence?).

If a fish is moving quickly at the surface it is not doing so in order to exhaust itself. There are, no doubt, exceptions. There are village idiots among fish, just as there are village idiots among men. But in the main, as we have discussed, fish move just as fast as they have to, and no faster. And if a trout is consistently moving at high speed at the surface (and even more certainly, if several fish are moving at high speed at the surface) it is because it is having to do so in order to catch a prey which is either itself moving at high speed, or which the fish knows from either experience or instinct, is *capable* of moving at high speed, and escaping.

The most common fly that causes the trout to move briskly upon it is the sedge or caddis.

Many species of caddis are large, as flies go, and are therefore tempting on this ground alone. But some species of caddis set up an enormous commotion on the water when they hatch; or when they scutter across the surface, to lay their eggs.

The scuttering V-wake of the latter, and the flutterings that the former creates, awake the predatory instincts of nearby fish; and the capacity – whether latent or apparent – for high speed movement on the part of the fly results in a high-speed response on the part of the trout.

Because the sedges are in the main nocturnal creatures – they tend to hatch in the evenings, and lay their eggs in the evenings – then the slashing rise is most commonly an evening phenomenon. If there is a slashing rise during the day, then the angler who knows the night-time predilections of most of the sedges will turn his mind to other beasts. And the candidate highest on the list will be a large terrestrial insect that has deposited itself upon the surface or, of course, during its relatively short season, the Mayfly.

The waggle

The "waggle" – for want of a more elegant though less descriptive term – is not a common rise-form. It is, however, important to draw attention to it, so that it can be distinguished from the head-and-tail rise earlier described.

The waggle is a rise-form in which the shoulders, dorsal fin and tail of the fish are visible in the surface film, almost simultaneously. It is a phenomenon of smooth water of uniform flow; and denotes a fish feeding – often besottedly – on small ephemeropteran duns and spinners drifting down in flotillas upon the current.

It is a languid rise: a rise clearly made by a fish that has had a good sighting of its prey, and that has simply drifted up into the surface from its position just below. It is a rise made by a fish that has almost lain in wait for the fly to drift into its mouth. There is the merest trace of forward propulsion as the fish, mouth closing and turning down from the horizontal, shrugs his way below the film again.

The last part of the trout's anatomy to disappear is its tail. Someone, a long time ago, described the languid shrug as "a satisfied wag of the tail". It is an apt and accurate description, for more than one reason. The trout has acquired his natural fly, and not taken our artificial. The waggling trout rarely gets caught on the artificial fly, in our experience.

The plain rise

The "plain" rise is the straightforward removal of a dun or other creature, from the surface of the water.

It is a plain, unromantic, unexotic rise that does not have outstanding characteristics: no sips or kisses, no slashes at the surface, no languid rolls. It is a rise for all seasons – an Ombudsrise – and it can occur almost anywhere. The trout simply sees the fly – usually a dun – swims up to it, opens its mouth and takes it in, before rolling away.

The plain rise occurs in both swift water and slow, and the manifestations of it will change with the character of the water.*

In slow water, there will be a positive, circular, ebbing of rings, occasionally accompanied by an audible smacking noise. In fast, rippled water there will be a peremptory interruption of the flow, combined with a brief cross-ripple similar to that described for a nymphing fish in fast water – though more pronounced. In water that is swift and unbroken the rise will show immediately as a ring, but will then be swept away to nothingness, in a yard or two.

In other words, the basic movement of the fish is consistent, and only the water changes. In the creation of many of the more specialized rise-forms it is the movement of the fish that alters.

There is one last point that we would make, that is important to the observation of rise-forms in general, and surface rise-forms in particular. There is one characteristic clue that the surface-feeding fish leaves behind that

*All rises, of course, are to some extent dependent upon the character and speed of the water and, indeed, upon the amount of fly available, and the depth at which the fish is lying. It is interesting to note that these factors can lead to different kinds of specific rise-form even when only one kind of fly is involved – the dead or dying fly trapped in the surface film. On slow reaches, close to the bank, the typical rise to such creatures in a heavy "fall" would be the "sip" rise: the "sip" tends to be more characteristic of trout lying close to the bank. In midstream, where the water is somewhat faster, the fish taking such creatures in a heavy fall will probably rise with a head-and-tail motion, or perhaps with a "waggle". If the fall is sparse, however, then a "plain" rise will ensue: the fish seeking food that is only sparsely available will lie deeper to give himself a wider field of view. And his trajectory and speed in coming up from the depths and returning to them creates a more vigorous disturbance than that made by his longitudinal friend mentioned above. The head-and-tail, the "sip" and the "waggle" are all created by fish lying close to the surface where the fish has a small field of view. They are, therefore, suggestive of fish with plenty of fly passing over them – and so all are rises seen in heavy hatches or falls.

the sub-surface feeder does not. It is a clue that can help to separate the two, when the rise itself goes unobserved.

It is: bubbles.

When a trout takes a fly from the surface, it cannot help but take in some air as well. When a trout does take in air, it gets rid of it as rapidly as it can, by opening its gills. And because the trout is well below the surface when the gills are opened, the air rises to the surface as a bubble or bubbles.

In calm water, therefore, if the light is awkward and it is difficult to see whether the rise has been through the surface film or just below it – look for the tell-tale bubbles. (But beware, of course, of grayling. Grayling almost always leave bubbles because of the speed of their rise, and the abruptness with which they turn at the surface, to return to the depths.)

The myth of the kidney-shaped whorl

The greatest liberator of the human mind in fly-fishing this century was G.E.M. Skues. That is our view. From the time he first appeared in print in a letter to *The Field* in the 1890s, to his death in the late 1940s, Skues brought more insight, perception and commonsense to fly-fishing literature than any other angler of whom we know or have heard.

But understandably, in the course of such a long and communicative life, there are some points on which Skues was mistaken – or mistaken, at least, in our view. We will touch upon one of these points now, because it has passed into the folklore of fly-fishing: and in particular, into the folklore of English fly-fishing.

That point is the cause of what Skues described as the "kidney-shaped whorl", a name he gave to the rise-form he associated with the Blue-Winged Olive so beloved of the chalk-stream angler (Fig. 22).

Since Skues described this rise-form and its "characteristic" kidney-shaped double-whorl, two generations of anglers to date – as no doubt will several to come – have scanned the water for it, when the BWO has been expected. The kidney-shaped whorl has become a "classical" rise-form, like the sip or the slash.

What the eye has not seen, the mind has imposed; and the supposed observation of it, has led to the hasty delivery of the BWO in its artificial form.

There is no such rise-form as the kidney-shaped whorl. More precisely, a disturbance not unlike a kidney shape may occasionally be made by a feeding fish – but such a disturbance *is characteristic of nothing*, ninety-nine times out of a hundred. The one-hundredth time, a kidney-type shape may appear on the water surface, but that will have been created by a fish that has risen to one fly, turning away at the last moment to take another. The so-called kidney-shaped displacement of water occurs no more frequently as a response to a particular insect, than as any other contortion of the water surface that the observer might dignify with a name.

When a fish moves to intercept a fly, it displaces water. And it is true that there is a direct relationship between the speed of the fish, and the violence

Fig. 22 The Blue-Winged Olive—the cause of more confusion in angling literature, than would have been created by water flowing uphill.

with which the water is disturbed. But the disturbance itself can and does take on almost *any* shape, give or take a broad circular movement that is influenced by the current, once the action is over.

There is no species of insect that would require a fish to move in a way that would consistently result in a kidney-shaped whorl, any more than there is, say, a species of sedge that would result in the eruption of the slashing rise taking on, say, a crown shape, or a steeple shape, or a ship shape.

However, the kidney-shaped whorl is now imprinted upon the mind of the fly-fisher. It is a handy picture that he can see in his mind's eye and often *expects to see* on the water. The deception is a self-deception, very close indeed to the kind of process through which the trout apparently goes when he expects to see a fly, and rises to something with a nasty sharp hook inside it.

Happily, the results are less severe. If they were not, indeed, there would be very few fly-fishers left – and no fishers to the rise to the BWO, at all.

JG fishes to a trout in the margins

PART TWO

Vision

Trout and man

6 How the trout sees

In the first part of this book we have considered the trout and his environment from the dry seclusion of our position on the bankside. To the layman standing on the edge of a clear stream or lake, wherein every weed and stone is clearly visible, there might seem no good reason why one should go further: why the trout looking upwards should not have a similar view to the one that we have looking downwards – though, of course, in reverse.

The fact is, however, that there are several good reasons why the trout does not, and cannot, see things as we see them; and an excursion below the surface will not only give the observer new insights into trout behaviour, but a better understanding of the angling techniques that he might employ.

In view of its profound importance to the angler, it is surprising to us that the great mass of angling literature has ignored the question of fish vision, and the factors which influence it.

The first author to touch upon the subject, briefly, was Alfred Ronalds in *The Fly-Fisher's Entomology*, published in the middle of the nineteenth century. Since then only a handful of writers have looked at fish vision in any detail. The most notable of these have been Dr Francis Ward in *Animal Life Under Water* (1919) – a book that was far ahead of its time; J.W. Dunne in *Sunshine and the Dry Fly* (1924) – an interesting and unusual work; Col E.W. Harding in *The Fly-fisher and the Trout's Point of View* (1931) – much the most thorough study of the subject published up to that point; and E.R. Hewitt in *A Trout and Salmon Fisherman for Seventy-five Years* (1948). More recently a beautiful book published in the United States by Vincent Marinaro – *In the Ring of the Rise* – has discussed aspects of the subject; and *Through the Fish's Eye* by Mark Sosin and John Clark, also published in the United States, likewise should be mentioned.

But when one has said that, one has said most of it. It is also important to note that even those books that have discussed the subject – including some of those mentioned above – have incorporated either basic misunderstandings that have led their authors to some incorrect conclusions, or else have been based upon a level of scientific knowledge which has since been superseded – again leading their authors to some incorrect conclusions (or, at least, to conclusions which appear to be incorrect today: one thing no-one can yet say is how the brain of a fish *interprets* the messages transmitted from the eyes).

Light, the "window" and the "mirror"

Any discussion of what the trout can see – and of the relevance of this to angling technique – can only sensibly begin with an examination of the means by which the trout sees anything.

Such a discussion will focus on *light* (without which nothing could be seen by anything); and the capacities of the fish's eye itself. The former will take us into the world of the "window" and the "mirror"; and the latter, given today's knowledge of the structure and physics of the eye, will give us an appreciation of what the trout is capable of seeing in that world.

Light is the medium by which anything is seen; and in the natural world of

Fig. 23 These photographs demonstrate clearly the effects of the refraction or bending of light. The mark on the stick is half way down its length, and the stick itself is touching the bottom. In the photograph on the left, refraction makes the stick appear to be shorter than it actually is. Because therefore we know that the end of the stick is further away than it seems, we know that the river or lake bed is also further away: in other words, *the water is deeper than appearances might suggest.*

In the photograph on the right, the bending of light is made visible. The stick, of course, is straight, but it appears to bend sharply where it cuts through the surface. One of the most practical effects of refraction for the angler—when he is trying to judge the exact position of a trout in the water—is made clear by Fig. 24.

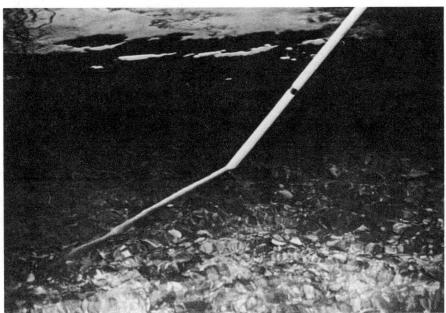

the outdoors, all light originates from the sun. It comes to us as a continuous wave, but for our purposes here is best described as an infinite number of individual "rays".

It is these rays which carry the images of our surroundings into our eyes, and enable objects to be seen.

These rays of light from the sun travel in a straight line through the air (which is not a dense medium) until they reach the water (which is). Then, at the point at which they enter the water, they bend. Anyone who has thrust a stick into the water will have seen it foreshorten or bend. This is the refraction of light, made visible (Fig. 23, and note Fig. 24).

However, not all rays of light are capable of entering the water to the same extent. The lowest rays to carry a useful image to any given point below the surface (for example, the eye of a trout) coincide with the surface at an angle of about 10 degrees to the horizontal.*

The very lowest rays bend where they enter the water at an angle of approximately 48.5 degrees to the vertical. Rays entering the water *above* 10 degrees to the horizontal, bend less and less until they reach a single ray that falls into the water from directly overhead, and that does not bend at all. Figure 25 makes all of this clear.

Figure 25 also shows how, in a cross-section of the world of the trout, the only useful light that reaches the eye of the trout (or any other point below the surface) is contained within an *external* arc of some 160 degrees (180 degrees less the 10 degrees or so at either side that carry little useful light into the water); and anything outside the water that the trout sees clearly, must be contained within this arc.

*Although rays below 10 degrees *do* enter the water surface we are, in light of our experiments discussed on page 96, regarding 10 degrees as the effective cut-off point. So little light penetrates the water from below this level, that the images conveyed become ever darker and more meaningless.

Fig. 24 This diagram shows, in a figurative way, what refraction can mean to the angler. The angler sees his trout at position A—but the actual position of the trout is at B. In other words, fish appear to be lying less deep in the water than they really are.

Note also that if the bank went out to the point marked 'X', the angler would still see the fish, even though a straight line drawn between his eyes and the true position of the trout would now be cut off by the bank. Thus, refraction enables the angler to see around corners.

Alas, it also enables the trout to do the same!

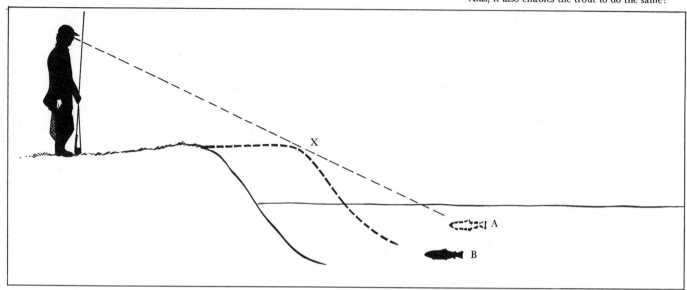

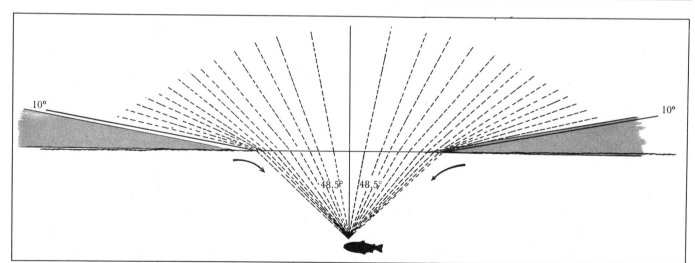

It is this field of view where it enters the water, that is known as the trout's "window". It is an appropriate choice of word: a "window" to the outside world.

The image that the trout receives through this window, is not a uniform one. It is obvious that if an external arc of approximately 160 degrees is compressed by refraction into an arc of approximately 97 degrees (Fig. 25 again) there must be a high degree of distortion. The greatest degree of distortion – which results in objects appearing shorter and consequently wider than they really are – occurs at the outside edge of the window, where the light rays are most bent and most compressed (see the photograph of the anglers on page 87).

Fig. 25 The external field of view of the trout (his "window"), showing how some 160 degrees of useful view outside the water, is funnelled down by refraction into 97° below water. The drawing is, of course, a cross-section: the trout sees all around it at the surface, and its window is circular. This diagram also gives a figurative impression of how the greatest crowding of rays of light occurs at the outside edge of the window, at the point at which they enter the water. It is this crowding and bending of rays that results in most of the images the fish receives around its window, being distorted.

Fig. 26 How the trout sees the world above the water. First, because only light that penetrates the surface from about 10 degrees or above carries useful images to him, any part of an external object that lies *below* 10 degrees is cut off at the 10-degree line, for all practical purposes.

Secondly, because the lowest rays of light bend where they enter the water and reach his eye at an angle of 48.5 degrees from the vertical, the trout sees *everything* from an angle of 48.5 degrees or less. He simply has no way of knowing that the angle outside the water is a mere 10 degrees. As a result, "ground level" to the trout is a permanent steep hill. This gives him the impression that most of what he can see outside is displaced to a point far above his head.

Note two other points: (a) because light coming to the trout from immediately overhead does *not* bend, the bird is neither displaced nor distorted; (b) outside the line going up from his eye at 48.5 degrees, the trout sees nothing of the outside world. *Everything* around his window is a mirror-image of the weeds and bottom around him.

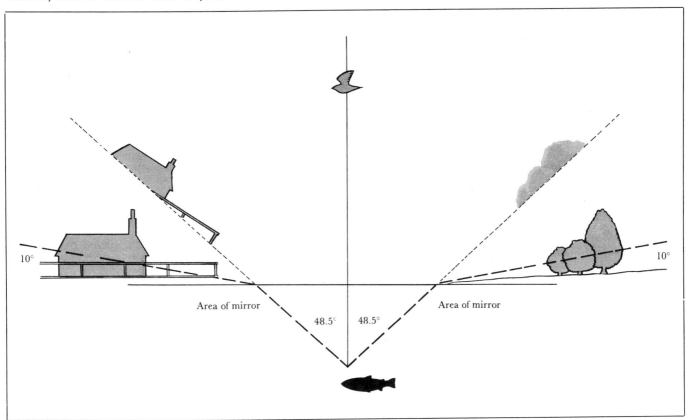

The distortion gets less and less until directly overhead (where, remember, the light does not bend) things are seen in true outline against the sky.

Figure 26 shows one other interesting point concerning the trout's view of the world above water. It is that because his "ground level" is light coming in at an angle of 48.5 degrees to the vertical, all the images that this light carries will be positioned at that angle above him. The effect is as though he were looking up a permanently steep hill with all the objects in the world outside displaced to a point far over his head.

Before moving on to the mirror, there is one last point that we would make. It is that because the angles of the cone of vision are fixed by the laws of refraction, they are constant. For the trout, the effect is that his window moves with him wherever he goes; and gets smaller in area as he nears the surface, and greater in area as he moves away from it (Fig. 27).

And now the "mirror". Because it is only through his window that he can see into the outside world, the trout is by definition surrounded by a large area of water surface through which he cannot see. When the water is calm and unbroken, this area reflects the world on the underside of the surface film; and it is this reflective area that has been dubbed – again appropriately – the "mirror".

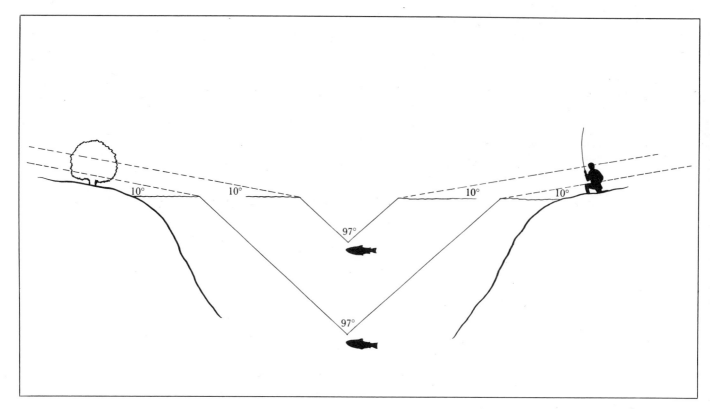

It should not be imagined that the mirror recedes into the distance like the ceiling of some vast, unsteady room. It does not. To the trout lying close to it, the mirror appears to slope sharply down around him like the roof of a bell-tent with its top sliced off. In front of him, the appearance is very like a cinema screen sloping down sharply to a horizon in the near middle-distance.

Because this optical effect places much of the mirror comfortably in front of the trout (and in the area which he can address with both eyes simultaneously) it seems likely that the mirror has more importance in his feeding behaviour than might at first be supposed. We touch upon some of the significances of this when fishing with nymphs, in the next chapter.

We would add just two important points on the mirror and the window, here. The first is that everything that we have discussed so far concerns the effects of optical laws. The figures that we have quoted can therefore be taken as fact. And because we have been discussing the effects of optical laws, the passages above have nothing at all to do with the properties of the eye of the trout. The trout is wholly subject to the phenomena discussed above, regardless of the properties of his eye.

The second point we would add is one of great importance to the angler. It is that the window and the mirror are separated by a fine circle of irridescent colours – a spectrum – that is known as Snell's Circle. In first observing this circle Mr Snell performed us all a great service, the full significance of which, so far as we can see, has been missed by everyone who has written on the fish's window and mirror, to date. This significance is discussed in some detail, later in this chapter.

The eye of the trout

There are a number of superficial similarities between the human eye, and the eye of the trout. Each, for example, has a cornea, an iris and a lens; and each has a retina carrying light-sensitive cells ("rods" and "cones") that detect the image that is formed upon them.

But that does not mean that the two eyes work in a similar way. Indeed, it

Fig. 27 The apex of the trout's cone of vision is fixed by the laws of refraction at 97 degrees, and so the area of the window will get smaller as the fish nears the surface, and greater as the fish moves away.

In theory, because some light enters the window from every point of the compass and from every level down to the horizontal, the trout's *field of view* will be constant regardless of the depth to which he swims. In practice, however, as we state elsewhere, very little light indeed enters the water from below an angle of 10 degrees to the horizontal. As a consequence, the lower trout in the diagram really can see more than his friend above.

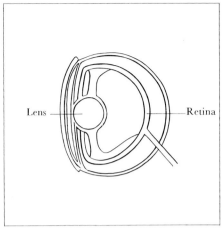

Fig. 28 The eye of the trout, with its powerful, spherical lens.

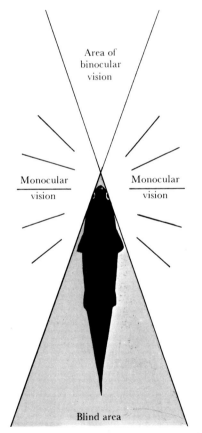

Fig. 29 The trout's range of vision. Because his wide-angle eyes are set into the sides of his head, there is only one small area in front of him where the fields of view that they encompass, overlap. It is this area of *binocular vision* that enables him to judge distance. On either side of his head, he can see only with the one eye that is facing in each direction. His monocular vision here is enough to alert him to movement, but he cannot tell how far away that movement is unless he turns full-face on, to look. The trout cannot see into the area behind him, because it is outside the range of either eye.

would be surprising, to say the least, if eyes that had evolved for use in utterly different media had ended up as much the same kinds of device.

The most significant differences of relevance to the angler lie in the shapes of the respective lenses, and in the means of focussing.

The reason why the two lenses and the focussing mechanisms have evolved so differently, can be readily understood from our discussion of refraction: from the fact that light travels in a straight line through one medium, and bends or refracts when it enters another medium of greater or lesser density.

For a man to see, light must pass from the rare medium of air into the dense fluid of the eye. In so doing, in obedience to the laws of refraction, it bends. The point of entry into the human eye is the curved cornea; and so it is here that considerable initial focussing, through refraction, occurs. The lens in the human eye simply acts as a fine-focussing device, on an image that has already begun to be formed.

In the case of the trout, things are very different. The light reaching him enters the fluid of his eye from another fluid all around it – the water. As a consequence, no significant refraction occurs at the point of contact, and so the cornea plays no real part in focussing an image. It is the *lens* of the fish that provides the sole means of focussing. It is to meet this burden that the lens of the trout has evolved into a very powerful mechanism indeed, compared with the lens of man. Whereas the lens in the human eye is fairly flat, the lens in the trout's eye has evolved into a sphere (Fig. 28).

Several points of great importance to the angler flow from this.

Because the lens of the fish is a sphere set into the side of its head, the trout has a field of view of some 180 degrees with each eye (Fig. 29). That much was hitherto well known.

What is not at all well known is that the trout can focus simultaneously on a whole range of objects on any given plane, right across this immense field of vision.

This marvellous facility is made possible by the way the light-sensitive cells – the rods and the cones – are grouped on the retina. In man, who only needs a narrow arc of concentrated focus because he can move his head from side to side to cover as wide an area as he wishes, the cones (which are responsible for the detection of colour and detail) are concentrated in a small area at the back of the retina – the fovea. In the case of the trout, which likewise needs a wide field of focus as a survival mechanism but which *cannot* move his head with such ease, the cones are distributed much more widely across his retina, as a compensating device. (The rods, which are responsible for vision in dim light and cannot detect either colour or detail, are much more evenly distributed over the retina in both man and fish.)

The ability of the trout to look and focus – literally – out of both corners of each eye simultaneously – is something that, to the best of our knowledge, has not been documented before in fly-fishing literature; and it has immense significance to the angler. It means that the fish can see – and in an active meaning of the term – in almost every direction at once. Even though, for example, he is looking intently at a fly advancing towards him on the current, he can see you advancing on his flank, with considerable ease. To say the least, this poses a fascinating picture of the kind of thing that must go on in the brain of the trout as he "juggles" with events being transmitted to him, and allocates them priorities of interest.

The trout's ability to see and focus through 180 degrees meets another need that any predator has – *binocular* vision. It is binocular vision that enables both the trout, and us, to judge *distance*. The trout obtains binocular vision in the area most important to him – directly in front, where his mouth is – from the fact that his two 180 degree eyes are positioned slightly towards the front of his head, where the frontal limits of the arc of vision can overlap. The penalty he pays for his binocular vision in front is that he has a corresponding blind area behind him.

Figure 29 makes clear how binocular vision is achieved in the trout.

Before moving on to the other specific aspects of trout vision, there is one more point that we wish to make about the trout's eye itself. It concerns the use that this remarkable mechanism can make of the available light.

Using the terminology that is employed to define the light-gathering capacities of photographic lenses, the human eye has been shown to have an effective aperture of approximately f2.0. By contrast, the effective aperture of the trout's eye has been shown to be approximately f1.2. This means (because the scale is inversely proportional, and the smaller the f number the greater the amount of light the lens admits) that if the eye of the trout were the same size as the eye of man, it would admit *four times* the amount of light. Even at the size that it is, it seems likely that the vision of the trout in poor light will be better than that of the angler pursuing him.

(It is a point of interest that the mathematics of fishes' eyes was worked out over 100 years ago by the physicist James Clerk Maxwell, whose curiosity was stimulated not by the trout, alas, but by the eye of his breakfast kipper!)

Focussing, and its relevance

It will be apparent from what we have already said that the trout's eye is a most remarkable device; one that has evolved to give him, among other capacities, a wide field of vision, binocular vision, almost all-round focussing and the rest. There is an aspect of this latter quality – his focussing – that is so interesting that we want to deal with it separately.

It concerns the fish's *depth* of focus, and the point at which his eye becomes focussed for "infinity".

If the reader feels that such considerations are over-technical and can have little practical significance, we would ask him to bear with us for a moment. The fact is that each of these considerations is of fundamental importance in the business of stalking a trout, and presenting it with a fly.

The principles of depth of focus or "depth of field" can best be established by referring again to the focussing mechanism of a modern camera with, say, its lens fully open (the trout cannot adjust its aperture like a camera lens, and so must always use its eye "fully open").

With a camera, there is a point at which it can be focussed (usually around

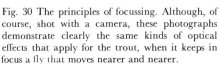

Fig. 30 The principles of focussing. Although, of course, shot with a camera, these photographs demonstrate clearly the same kinds of optical effects that apply for the trout, when it keeps in focus a fly that moves nearer and nearer.

Fig. 30A shows a view taken with the camera lens focussed for infinity. As will be seen, most of the view is in focus, and beyond a distance of about 30 feet, *everything* is in focus.

Fig. 30B shows the same view, with the camera lens now focussed much nearer (in fact, at about 4 feet). Note that the background has now become blurred, and that only a band in the near-foreground—across the middle of the stool—is in true focus.

Fig. 30C shows the view again, but this time with the lens focussed as closely as possible (about 18 inches distant). The entire picture has become blurred, with the exception of a narrow plane at the 18-inch mark, across the near side of the reel. At this distance, even the handle of the reel is out of focus.

When a trout is studying a fly perched at the end of his nose his view is similar to that in the last photograph, only very much more so. The depth of focus is even narrower, and the rest of his view is simply a deep grey mist that shows no detail whatsoever.

30 ft distant) beyond which *everything* comes into focus: the depth of field reaches to "infinity". As the lens is focussed nearer and nearer, the depth of field that is in focus gets less and less until, when the lens is focussed at the nearest point to which it *can* be focussed (usually about 18 inches) the depth of field is little more than paper-thick. Either side of that narrow plane, everything is out of focus. All of this is made clear by the photographs in Fig. 30.

Consider, now, the trout. All the observations that we have made so far about what he can see, and that other writers have tended to concentrate upon, have been based upon the assumption that the fish is focussed for infinity. That is clearly, for example, the only way he is going to see distant objects through his window.

But of course, the trout is *not* always focussed for infinity, any more than we are. And would it not be useful to know what is and is not in focus, when he is looking at objects at different distances? Indeed it would. Such information, for example, would tell us whether we are in focus at all, or so out of focus as to be invisible for all practical purposes *whether or not we are in his window*. Such information, likewise, would give us an insight into why one trout will move only an inch or two to intercept a fly drifting towards it, when another will move several feet: and so on.

We began with observation in the field.

We had already come to the conclusion that the trout was capable of focussing to within an inch, or a little more, of the end of his nose. We had studied hundreds of fish, on many different rivers, in many different circumstances, dropping downstream with their eyes that close to flies on the surface, and had no doubts about the internal limit of focussing, at all.

We had likewise come to the conclusion that fish feeding very close to the surface, had a very small depth of focus. In a heavy hatch of fly, the trout will take up station within two or three inches of the surface.

Such a fish will not move more than four or five inches to either side to take a fly. We concluded that the *absence* of such tiny lateral movements reflected the fact not so much that the fish was disinclined to shift, but that flies beyond this distance were invisible to him: that they were outside of his depth of field, when he was focussing on subjects so close to him.

We also noted that trout lying quite well down – say between 18 inches and 3 ft – would commonly move two, three, four and even five feet to intercept a fly or nymph. This seemed to indicate that when a trout was focussing at two feet or more his depth of field was enormously increased and, indeed, in all probability extended to infinity. When taken with the fish last mentioned above, it suggested that the point where the depth of field extends to infinity, occurred somewhere between 3 inches and two feet.

But we wanted, if we could get it, something more concrete than a series of simple deductions and we took the problem to Professor W.R.A. Muntz, of the Department of Biology at Stirling University. Professor Muntz has made a professional study of fish and fish behaviour and is, specifically, one of the world's leading authorities on fish vision.

Professor Muntz constructed for us the following table, based upon his work at the university and upon the assumptions that appear in the adjacent footnote.*

THE TROUT'S DEPTH OF ACCURATE VISION

Distance at which eye is focussed	1	2	3	4	6	10	15	20	23	25
Furthest distance at which accurate vision is possible	1.033	2.16	3.39	4.76	7.97	17.15	39.37	104.17	312.5	X

(All measurements in inches; X = infinity)

This table bears out our field observations to an almost startling degree; it would indeed seem that the point from which the trout can "see to infinity" occurs very close indeed to its eye, and in all probability occurs at something less than two feet.

One important point arising from this, and demonstrated by the table, concerns the question of stalking trout. Such practical observations as we

*It is assumed that the trout's eye has a diameter of half an inch, and that it is accurately focussed to the various distances shown in the top line of the table. It is also assumed that the fish will fail to recognize objects correctly when they are out of focus to such an extent that any point on the object is blurred into a circle 30 minutes across on the retina. A 10p piece at a distance of $10\frac{3}{4}$ feet is 30 minutes across, which gives some idea of the loss of image quality we have assumed: any point on an object (such as, for example, the cross-sectional tip of a rod) will appear to the trout as a blurred circle the size of the 10p piece. It is a point of interest that calculations were done for various other degrees of out-of-focus as well, with surprisingly little effect on the results.

have made, and the table above, suggest that where an angler finds a trout feeding within a very few inches of the surface, then he can approach that fish very much nearer than he could a trout feeding a foot or two deeper: he is likely to be out of focus to the fish feeding very high in the water, and is likely to remain undetected whether or not he falls within its window.

He should likewise note, however, that we are here discussing only *form*. There is nothing at all to say that because a fish cannot see an approaching angler's form very clearly, that it will not be able to detect his movement if he does not take care. And if the fish *is* alerted by a sudden, out-of-focus movement all he has to do is to alter focus, for the angler to come sharply into view.

Colour vision

Do freshwater fish, including trout, have colour vision? More particularly, perhaps, do they have the ability to distinguish between *different* colours? The answer, unequivocally, is yes.

There are many reasons for this certainty, including recent evaluation of the properties of the fish's eye by the use of electrodes to tap messages sent along the nerves from the eye to the brain. For the layman, however, all of that may be rather too chilling. The most simple and readily acceptable reason for believing that fish can see colour stems from the behavioural studies carried out on them, in laboratories.

Quite simply, in tests carried out in many laboratories in Britain, the United States, Germany and elsewhere, by scientists including Professor Muntz, fish have been *trained to respond* to different colours. Time and again, in demand-feeding experiments, they have shown that they can not only unerringly distinguish between different colours, but between different shades of the same colour. In such experiments, the fish get fed if they respond correctly to one colour, and they do not get fed if they respond to a different colour. Even the *sensitivity* of colour vision has been successfully tested, using this simple and well-tried formula: the fish are shown a "food" colour over and over but ever more weakly, until they simply fail to react to it.

It is interesting to note that, even given their small brains, the fish used in these experiments showed themselves to be quick learners. (Many of the fish Professor Muntz used in his experiments learned to distinguish between two colours in less than five trials: i.e. they made only one or two errors altogether!). It seems likely that the unerring selection of the correct colours by fish once trained, is not unconnected with the fact that almost half their brain is deployed in the use and control of the visual faculties.

What colours do fish see best? In fresh water, experiments have shown that the colour that fish see most easily is red. The next most visible colours are orange and yellow, in that order. The colours that fish see least easily are green and blue. These results have been obtained in conditions of normal light; they do not take account of the changes of colour that occur in very deep water.

Scientific studies have also shown that fish can see contrasting patterns or shades (particularly stripes, and to a lesser extent spots) with exceptional clarity. This may account to some extent for the effectiveness of the most popular wet flies on still waters – flies that incorporate red or orange in the body or tag, and that employ speckled feathers like teal and mallard, for the wing. Many such patterns come readily to mind – Peter Ross, Mallard and Claret, Parmachene Belle, Dunkeld, Teal and Silver, and many more besides. We would draw attention, however, to the careful wording we have used. The fact that certain colours or contrasts of colours are more conspicuous to fish, does not necessarily mean that fish are more attracted to them.

Night vision

Most writers seem to agree that trout are particularly wary and difficult to approach during the evening. While we would agree that this is true in the early evening, the reverse, in our experience, usually applies once the evening rise has commenced in earnest.

Our observations lead us to believe that the reason for the sudden transition from acute awareness to apparent unconcern, is less concerned with the trout's ability to see better than we can in most light, and much more closely linked with the trout's focus and feeding behaviour. That, and the fact that the light penetrating the surface and enabling the trout to see falls off sharply once the sun has set to the critical angle of 10 degrees to the surface.

Consider what happens. During the early part of the evening most trout take up lies in mid-water, and while a few individual fish may make odd forays to the surface to take the occasional dun or spinner floating down, the majority are merely observing, and waiting for the main hatch of dun or fall of spinner that normally occurs after the sun has set.

During this time, most trout are perhaps a couple of feet below the surface. At this depth, as already discussed, everything in the trout's window is in focus. What is more, because of the large aperture of his lens, also already noted, we know that in waning light he is likely to have better sight than the angler pursuing him. It is therefore not surprising that he is difficult to approach at this time: he can see well, because of his high-quality lenses; and all that he can see through his window is in focus.

As dusk approaches, however, the sequence of events discussed a page or so ago, sets in. The light reaching the fish gets rapidly less, and the fish moves closer and closer to the top, rising more frequently until, at the peak of the hatch, he is lying within a couple of inches of the surface. And the closer he moves to the surface, and the more he concentrates on it, the smaller his window gets and the more blurred distant objects in it become. And that includes the angler.

To facilitate an understanding of this sequence of events, and observations on the size of the window that we have made elsewhere in these chapters, we have compiled Fig. 31. It shows the diameter of window of the trout at various depths; and how the size of the window diminishes as the fish moves upwards.

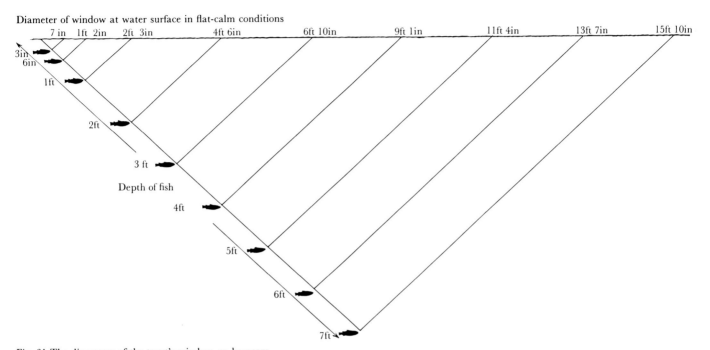

Diameter of window at water surface in flat-calm conditions

Fig. 31 The diameters of the trout's window, as he nears
and moves away from the surface. The figures are
accurate to the nearest inch.

7 What the trout sees of the fly

From what has already been said, the surface of the trout's world can be likened to a large, bell-tent-shaped mirror facing downwards – except that, in the centre, there is a circular area from which the silvering has been rubbed away.

This transparent circular area is the trout's window; and it is through this that he perceives the world above water. The window gets larger as he moves away from the surface, and smaller as he approaches it.

Let us now consider that most fascinating interrelationship: that between the trout and the surface fly.

The fly on the surface – and the "triggers" to the rise

Just as we cannot see through a mirror but only reflections *in* it, so it is with the trout. The trout can see nothing at all of the outside world through the mirror. In the area of the mirror, the only way that the trout can know that anything is present is where an object touches the surface film, or physically breaks through the surface film.

For this reason, when looking into the mirror, the trout can see the bodies of spent spinners and trapped terrestrial flies, *but not the bodies of most of the duns*.

The dead or dying spinner collapses spread-eagled onto the water surface, its wings trapped in that cloying glue. Immediately, its body breaks through the surface film, and the instant it does so, it becomes visible to the trout.

The dun in the mirror, however, stands aloft *on* the surface film, and its abdomen is largely kept clear by the legs and the natural upward arch of its body. The only means that the trout therefore has of spotting a distant dun floating on the mirror, is the tiny indentations that the fly's feet make in the surface film.

As shown clearly in the photograph on page 84, the feet of the dun create tiny star-bursts of light which the incredible eyesight of the trout is able to pick up from several feet away.

It is these star-bursts of light created by the indentations of the feet of the dun floating on the surface, that are the first trigger to the trout's predatory mechanism.

This trigger could be seen in action by large numbers of anglers if they were as concerned to observe a feeding trout and to learn from it, as they are to set about catching it at once. Time after time, a fish will be seen lying below the surface in a midwater feeding position – and to begin to rise at a time when the laws of refraction as discussed earlier, make it clear the fish cannot see the body or wings of the approaching fly at all: they fall below the critical angle of 10 degrees that the trout needs to reach his eye before he can see anything of value.

If nothing that we have said hitherto has convinced the sceptic that the trout has the most remarkable eyesight, surely it is this: the fact that in rapid, broken water, the trout can pick out those tiny indentations in the surface film, and launch himself on an upward trajectory with deadly precision. (Indeed, it is probable that it is the indentations of the feet of the fly, when coupled with the trout's remarkable eyesight, that enable the fish in some cases to feed selectively. It is probable, in light of observations that we have made, that the trout is able to distinguish between the different indentations in the film, made by flies of markedly different size, when these are on the water at the same time.)

The starburst of light from the feet of the dun on the surface of the mirror (or, of course, the light refracted down from the struggles of a terrestrial fly or spinner) is not the only trigger that the trout's primitive predatory mechanisms have – although, in our opinion, it is by far the most important. There is a second trip-mechanism: the *wings* of the fly.

Consider a dun floating on the surface, in the mirror, towards the trout (or, if the trout is in a lake, consider a trout swimming towards the fly – the principle is exactly the same).

The fly, whose body is invisible to the fish, gradually gets nearer to the lowest rays of light which carry clear images of the outside world, down into the window of the trout. First the wings cut through those rays (Fig. 32) and they appear, disembodied, up the "hill" on which everything the trout sees is positioned.

Fig. 32 How the trout sees a dun approaching. The wings come into view first, "flared" over the edge of the window while the abdomen is still over the mirror. The abdomen itself does not come into view and join the disembodied wings until it also enters the window. It is *only* from the edge of the window onwards, that the trout can see the whole fly.

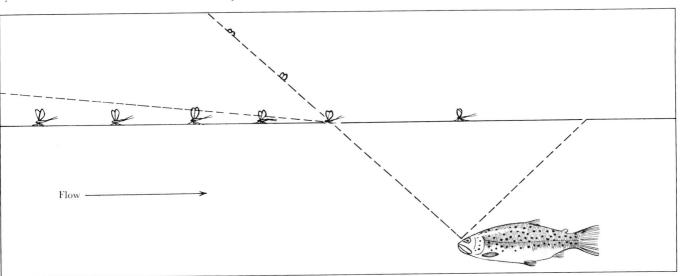

Gradually, more and more of the wings become visible as they cut through those lowest rays of "visible" light. Finally, as the body of the fly reaches the edge of the trout's window and itself is encompassed by the lowest rays, the body and wings *both* become visible, and the whole of the dun can be seen.

The speed of the process, of course, depends upon the rate of the current on the river, or the rate of approach of the trout in the lake; but in practice it happens smoothly and quite quickly, and the flaring effect of the wings from the position of the trout can be likened to a lighted, high-pressure gas jet: under full pressure, the flame appears some distance away from the aperture of the jet, but gradually, as the pressure is diminished, it gets nearer and nearer until it "joins" the jet itself.

The whole process of transition from the feet impressions in the mirror, to the flaring of the wings over the edge of the window, is made clear by the photographs on pages 84 and 85. It is largely because of this flaring effect that we believe that wings in floating flies (see later) can be helpful when addressing sophisticated trout.

Colour in the surface fly

We have already established that the trout can see colour, and have shown how the surface fly becomes visible to the fish from below water. Let us now draw these two together, and consider what the trout can see of the *colour* of the surface fly.

The spent spinner, or any other fly whose body breaks through the surface film, is the most briefly summed up.

As already discussed, the trout can see clearly anything that penetrates the mirror; and because he has excellent colour vision, he can see the colour of whatever has penetrated the mirror, as well. As a consequence, colour in the body of the spent spinner and terrestrial flies is clearly of importance to the fly-fisher.

The fly floating *on* the surface, however, is a much more complex proposition. Let us consider again the fly floating towards the trout, that we discussed a moment ago.

First of all, the fish sees the feet in the surface film. But under normal conditions the feet do not transmit colour – simply sparkles of white light. The first that the trout sees of the fly itself is when the wing-tips "flare" over the edge of his window. As the trout can see colour, and can by definition see through his window, the colour of the wings is therefore also a matter that the angler must consider. In the conventional artificial fly, as a consequence, the colour of the *hackles* becomes particularly important because it is these which "flare" over the edge of the trout's window, in the manner of wings. It is, it should be noted, the hackles that are important even when a fly is tied with wings as well: the colour of the hackle drowns the colour of the wings, because the hackle reflects light more effectively.

As the body of the fly progresses from the mirror towards the window of the fish, it passes through the fine dividing-line between the two – the prismatic ring known as Snell's Circle. For a brief moment in and beside that prismatic ring, when the sun is overhead or behind the trout, the whole colour of the fly – wings *and* body – can be seen. Once through Snell's Circle, the fly passes further and further into the centre of the window, becoming darker against the brilliant light overhead, as it goes. Most of this is made plain by the photographs on page 83.

For most fish, therefore, we are convinced that while the colour of the hackle and/or wings on the dun *does* have importance, colour in the body is of less consequence, and the prime requirements of a successful floating fly – after the creation of suitable feet dimples – are correct size, silhouette and (to a certain degree) translucency.

Note, however, that we said for most fish and not for all fish. We believe that correct size and silhouette are the most important characteristics when fishing to the average trout, because the average trout is not a very discriminating beast. A well-dressed fly presented in a natural way to a steadily feeding fish will catch it nine times out of ten. The reason, we believe, is that the trout is programmed to recognize a series of generalities only – and when he sees them, *he reacts unless he has learned better*.

The average, inexperienced trout commits himself to the rise, in our experience, from the moment he sees the first of the generalities – the dimple patterns made by the feet in the mirror. That is why the conventional fly works – it shows him what he wants or expects to see. In particular, it shows him the first of his two key trigger-points: the hackles with which the fly is wound make light patterns in the surface film broadly similar to the light patterns made by the feet of the natural dun. As he therefore ascends to take the conventionally-hackled fly, the trout has already "recognized" in it what he is looking for; and if he should pause briefly before consuming it, he will have his conviction reinforced: he will see its hackles flare over his window-edge, for all the world like the wings he would also "expect" to see.

(It is an aside, but there can be little doubt that many trout never actually see the body of the fly that catches them, at all. If the fish is confident and unafraid, it will begin its rise as soon as the light dimples in the mirror are sighted. Then, if its ascent is at the same rate as that at which the fly is approaching, its window will decrease in advance of the fly. The fly as a consequence will be "held" in the mirror, right up to the point at which it topples or is sucked into the mouth of the fish.)

Colour and the experienced fish

And what of the experienced fish – the fish that has seen it all before; that is *not* content to commit its soul to a starburst of hackle-points on the surface film? For this fish, we believe that everything has to be right, *including body colour*.

Why body colour? Let us go back yet again, to the fly floating towards an experienced trout on the current. The fish sees the indentations of the feet, and begins to rise upwards to intercept. But not for him a mad, impulsive rush; he drifts up slowly and purposefully, in such a way as the fly, as he ascends, moves steadily from the mirror into his window. The wings begin to flare, and then to join up with the abdomen of the fly, on the very edge of his window.

In the normal course of events, the artificial fly would move quickly across the rim, and would darken swiftly into a silhouette against the light above. *But the wary, experienced fish, does not allow it to do so.* Indeed, why on earth should he? We have already discussed how the window is surrounded by a fine circular prism, and that it is only when the fly is in or very close to this, that the fish can see the colour of the fly in all its detail.

When the sunlight is not behind the fly, to turn it into a silhouette the moment it appears, the experienced fish rises until the fly is on the edge of his window, and can be seen in full colour. Then, the trout drops downstream with the fly, holding it there until he is satisfied that it is exactly what he wants (Fig. 33). Only then will he rise. More commonly (it is why he has survived so long, and has become an experienced fish) he will not.

We have seen hundreds of experienced trout dropping downstream in this way, "locked on" to natural flies as well as artificials. The fly is held within an inch or two of the fish's nose, in fine focus, while the whole scrutiny process goes on.

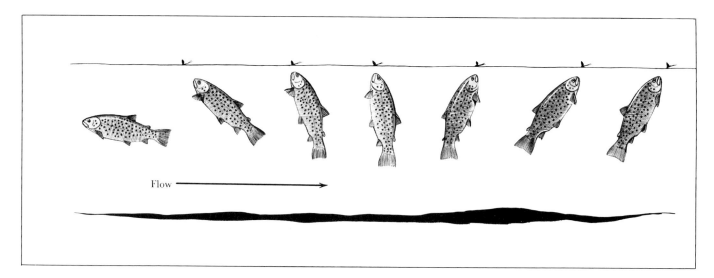

Fig. 33 Colour in the artificial fly *can* be important. An experienced fish will "lock on" to a fly when it enters the narrow area of close-up colour vision that surrounds his window, and hold it there as he drops downstream with it. The distance at which a suspicious fish keeps the fly rarely seems to vary.

We are quite sure that fish behaving in this way are using the full powers of vision and self-preservation that the good Lord has given them. Indeed, we do not believe it to be improbable that highly suspicious fish shift sufficiently below the fly to move it in and out of the window and prism, assessing in this way not simply colour, but form as well – and over and again in a single drift.

It was to meet the demands of these special fish, that we developed the range of duns and spinners which follow at the end of this book. They have been designed to give the experienced fish almost everything that we believe it could want: a body (in the case of the dun) which stands aloft from the surface film; a body (in the case of the spinner) which lies in the surface film; feet indentations in the mirror; wings to flare over the edge of the window; appropriate coloration; accurate profile in the window; matching size.

We do not believe that the hook is a great deterrent to the trout – and quite clearly to 99 trout out of a hundred it is no deterrent at all. In setting out to meet the requirements above, we found, nonetheless, that we had in some instances to remove the hook bend from the water to the air, and the trout do not seem to miss it much.

We have taken many fish of the kind just discussed, with such dressings. They are not infallible, any more than any artificial fly is likely to prove infallible (indeed, if an infallible fly *were* to be developed, millions would leave the sport after half a dozen outings; and the fish would go with them). The new dressings are, however, a most useful *supplement*, presenting the angler with a number of advantages over the conventional fly, when those advantages are most sorely needed: when he is confronted with difficult, experienced, desirable and often *large* trout, that turn up their imperious noses at wound-hackle flies.

As a footnote, we would add one last point. Any trout will be made that much more difficult to catch if its suspicions are aroused. A careful, unobserved approach, and a delicate and accurate first cast, will do more to catch even an experienced fish than almost any refinement of the fly.

Recognition of the sub-surface fly

Away from the dazzling and brilliantly coloured world of the surface, with its sunlight and its prisms, the world of the trout becomes a different place. The background is one of dull greens and browns and shadows and blurs; and the creatures which live there, and on which the trout feeds, are clad in similar hues.

In the greenish fastnesses of still water, the trout has no current to bring food to him; and so he must hunt it. In the hunting, he is obliged to rely a great deal on the movement and profile of his well-camouflaged prey, to help him to spot it. One of the reasons that coloured artificial flies attract so much attention from trout on lakes is because the trout sees colour in an unadulterated way and – most importantly – because such flies are fished with *movement*.

On rivers, while the occasional fish will rummage his way among the stones and the gravel and the weeds, for the most part the trout is content to let the current bring his food to him. He hangs on the current, and relies on his powerful eyesight to help him to make quick judgments on what is and is not food, on the vast conveyor-belt all around him.

In coloured water and fast currents, the trout does not see any object until it is close up, and then he must make a quick decision on whether or not it is food. It seems likely, therefore, that his judgments under conditions such as these are based upon size, upon a quick impression of shape, and upon "life" as suggested by movement of legs and other appendages.

For trout in fast and coloured water, therefore, precise imitation cannot be essential; and there can be little doubt, for example, that the North Country spider patterns succeed not because they actually *look* like food, but because their soft, clinging hen hackles create in a hazy, impressionistic way, the qualities that the trout is hoping to see.

In the clearer and generally slower water of the chalk streams and limestone rivers, the trout can see further, see more detail, and see it longer. Accurate representation is therefore much more important, and the most successful sub-surface patterns on clear water streams are those that both *look* like the natural creature, and *behave* like the natural creature.

This, of course, is why Sawyer's Pheasant Tail Nymph, the Sunken Spinner and our shrimp dressings are so deadly. And that is why we believe there is enormous scope for the further imitation of the subaqueous food of river trout. (Precise imitation is by no means *always* necessary – and in addressing most fish we are inclined to functionalism in our nymphs. But there is, nevertheless, much interest and pleasure to be obtained from refinements in this field, by those prepared to seek it.)

Significance of the mirror

As though the clearer and less turbulent water of the chalk stream and limestone river were not sufficient advantage, some trout which live in such comfortable surroundings have yet another aid to their subaqueous feeding: an aid shared only with the trout which hunt for nymphs, shrimps and their kin in the shallows of clear, calm lakes. They have the *mirror*.

We mentioned when discussing the optics of the underwater world in which the trout lives, that the mirror is not like the ceiling of a vast room that recedes into the distance. It appears, instead, rather like the walls of a bell-tent that hang diagonally down around him. And because, as we said earlier, this optical effect places the mirror comfortably in front of him, it seems probable that in calm, shallow water the trout not only looks for the feet indentations of flies in the mirror, and their bodies trapped in it, as already discussed. Because the hanging screen of the mirror reflects everything on its underside, it seems highly likely that the trout addresses himself to it for reflections as well: for the movements of aquatic creatures wriggling their way up from the bottom, and along the bottom. By concentrating upon the mirror around or in front of him, the trout is able to see creatures that fall both above and below a line of concentrated vision directed elsewhere: in other words, the mirror provides him, in calm conditions, with a far wider range of view than it might at first be supposed he has.

For the river fisherman, who seldom finds himself on water free of surface distortion, such observations might appear interesting but not widely applicable. For the man who fishes lakes, however, there is a point to be made.

Because the mirror *is* a mirror, it reflects that side of any object or creature which is facing towards it. The mirror in a calm lake, therefore, reflects the *back* of any creature which is moving below it: and what is more, it reflects that back against the sombre green-and-brown background of the reflected bottom. Nymphs for fishing shallow lakes in flat calm might therefore be designed with an awareness of this.

Because of the reflective properties of the mirror, and the likelihood that in calm water the trout uses the advantages it gives him when hunting nymphs and other subaqueous food, there seems to be an excellent case for incorporating into the dressings of some stillwater nymphs a tiny strip of white feather-fibre or silver lurex, mounted flat along the back.

Such a device would mean that the spot of light would be there, to attract attention against the dark background of the mirror – but size, profile and general coloration would be preserved, and would aid deception when the nymph is addressed by the trout with direct vision.

In the world of the trout

The pages which follow include many unusual photographs taken to illustrate points we have made in the text concerning trout feeding behaviour and trout camouflage. They also include a sequence of high-speed pictures showing the capture of one particularly large fish.

All of these photographs were taken in the wild, without artificial aids or contrivances of any kind. They do, therefore, represent a true record of actual events, as they occurred.

Feeding Behaviour

As discussed in detail in the text, there is a close link between the movement of the trout, and the movement of the creature it is hoping to eat. And, of course, there is a close relationship between the movement of the trout, and the water it displaces, (the "rise-form"). Learning to trace back from the rise-form he observes, to the insect the trout is eating, is perhaps the most important step that the fly-fisher can take.

Left: No need to hurry . . . A quiet rise – usually accompanied by a brief sipping or kissing noise – is almost always made to flies trapped in or immediately under the surface film, that the fish knows from experience cannot get away.

Above: A high-speed slash, as a big trout hurls itself after a departing sedge. No creature in the wild expends more energy than it has to, and a violent rise-form like this is almost always to a large insect that the trout knows could easily escape.

Left: The trickiest rise of all to distinguish . . . and it's easy to see why. The lunge of the trout as it removes a nymph from the underside of the surface film, creates a disturbance that is almost identical to the typical rise to surface fly. Only careful observation will reveal the truth.

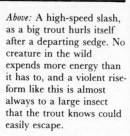

Left: Here the trout has intercepted the ascending nymph a little way below the surface. The whorl it has created is typical of the rise-form created by fish taking nymphs close to the surface. The other common surface disturbance such fish make is a brief welling-up or "bulging" of the surface film.

Left: A fascinating aspect of underwater feeding . . . a trout using the flat side of its mouth to shovel up a shrimp clinging determinedly to the bottom. (Note the photograph of the shrimp-eating trout later in this colour section.)

Left: Not all fish become "preoccupied" with food close to the surface. This trout has adopted the characteristic attitude of a fish hunting on the bottom for caddis larvae, stonefly nymphs, shrimps and the like.

Below: Perhaps the most languid, classical rise-form of all, the head-and-tail rise, a feeding pattern typical of the trout intercepting small duns, and some spinners and nymphs trapped by the surface film. Here the tail of the fish waves its contemptuous goodbye.

Below: The push of a tail, a leisurely realignment, and a nymph disappears from the stream. The split-second blink of white as the trout opens his mouth is one of the most important clues that the observant nymph fisherman looks for, in helping him to pinpoint his quarry.

Camouflage

The trout is a master of camouflage, and can change
subtleties of his coloration from reach to reach and even
from lie to lie.

Left: A grey shade holding
station in a typical lie –
ahead of an obstruction
rising from the riverbed.

Left: The camouflage of
some trout is so perfectly
matched to their
surroundings that only the
most practised and
penetrating eyes will pick
them out. In this picture
there is a large trout
immediately in front of the
arrow.

Below: The blink of the
camera-shutter catches a
trout just below the
surface, in the back-eddy of
a waterfall – and in so
doing, makes the presence
of the fish appear much
more obvious than it
otherwise would have been.
When the water is in
motion, and the surface
reflection is changing
constantly like this, trout
can be very difficult indeed
to see.

Left: Riding the deep, dark
water beneath a bridge,
ready to sink softly out of
sight.

The world under water

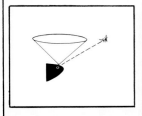

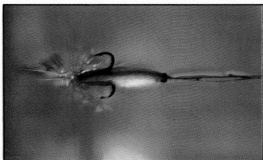

The first sight that the trout gets of the fly is when he sees it in the mirror as it approaches him (or, on stillwaters, as he swims towards it). If, as in the case on the left, the body of the fly penetrates the surface film, the fish can see the body colour; otherwise (see overleaf) all he can see is the feet of the fly, where they touch the surface. Note how the mirror's reflection shows the fish two hooks, not one.

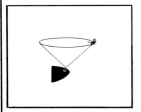

The fly is now passing over the rim of the window (note sky appearing at the top). This is a photograph of profound importance to the angler. Most writers have argued that only size and shape are important in the artificial . . . that the fish sees only a silhouette in its window. In fact the full colour of the artificial fly is visible to the trout: the fish has a narrow circle of full colour vision around the edge of its window, whether or not the body of the fly penetrates the surface film. . . . and many trout hold the fly in this circle, to study it more closely.

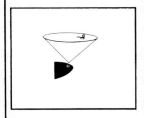

The fly begins to enter the window – and to lose its colour. From this point on, colour is less important. Even the body of the spinner, which lies *in* the surface film (unlike the dun, which stands *on* the surface film) loses colour as it moves across the window.

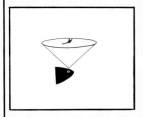

Now the fly is directly overhead. At this point, the trout can see comparatively little colour: the fly has become a near silhouette against the light. (Note that our comments above concern the appearance of the artificial fly against the light. Under some circumstances some natural flies become translucent when seen in the window).

The triggers to the rise

1 – THE FEET IN THE FILM

REVEALED . . . exactly what it is that the
feeding trout looks for, that triggers his
predatory mechanisms, and that launches him
on his way to the surface.

On this page . . . the tiny
indentations that the feet of
the advancing fly make in
the mirror. As discussed in
the text, the trout cannot
see *through* the mirror, and
so cannot see the fly itself.
But that tiny starburst of
light from the feet warns
him that a fly is on its way.
Who now, having watched
fish rising in turbulent
water, can believe the trout
has less than perfect vision?

Left: On the edge of the
window, where he can see
the fly as well.

Left: In the window, and
as the fly assumes its
familiar silhouette, the
dimples of the feet become
dark.

2 – THE WINGS IN THE WINDOW

The confirming signal to the rising trout is the extraordinary "flaring" of the wings as they float, disembodied, over the rim of the window . . . eventually to join up with the abdomen. The wings begin the "flare" while the fly is still some distance away from the trout – as evidenced by the top picture opposite.

Most trout do not wait for this second signal, but commit themselves from the moment they see the indentations of the feet. Experienced trout, however, almost invariably do. They rise with great deliberation, and wings can sometimes mean the difference between failure and success.

In this picture *(left)* , the bodies of the flies are in the mirror (note the double image of the fly on the right) . . . but the effects of refraction are already revealing the wings in the window of the trout.

Left: The wings and the bodies are getting closer together, as the fly itself is carried towards the window.

Left: The moment of union. The wings and the bodies come neatly together on the edge of the window. Note that in every case with these flies the bodies are visible throughout, because they have sunk into the surface. This is one of the most common causes of failure with the traditionally-dressed fly. In the photographs opposite, for which we used our new dressings, the body is kept clear of the surface, as is the case with most natural duns. Note, too (see pages 148–157) how the new dressings that we have devised, incorporate the triggers of both the feet and the wings – and keep the hook clear of the water.

Technical truths

What colour of floating flyline is best? All the debate on flyline colour has concentrated on appearances in the air, and on the water in the window. The photograph below reveals the truth . . . that it is not the line in the air or in the window that should be considered, but the line on the water *in the mirror*. The white flyline, although it causes a degree of flash (right) in the air, is most of the time less visible to the trout. But it falls like a flash of white lightning across all the water surrounding the trout . . . across the mirror. There can be little doubt, as a consequence of our experiments and photographs such as the one below, that white or light-coloured flylines should not be used when the trout are close to the surface.

Above: How a green and a white line in the air, appear to the trout through his window. While the darker line is in the main more easily seen, the score is evened-up by the occasional flash the white line gives off (note lower-right of the picture).

Left: Why – even when fishing the surface fly – the leader should never be greased close to its end. Of the three leaders shown, the least visible is the centre one, treated to sink. The leader on the left was simply wiped clean. The leader on the right was dressed with a flotant.

Left: Rod-flash shows even more clearly in colour than it does in black and white (see page 97). It is quite clear that the reflection of bright sunlight off gloss varnish must alert many trout, whether or not the angler is aware of it at the time.

Below: How a wading angler appears to the trout – and a theory disproved. Ever since angling writers have begun to investigate trout vision, it has been believed that the trout approached by a wading angler must see four legs – the real legs, and their reflection in the mirror. This picture was one of several dozens we took with a camera sunk into the bed of the river. No legs at all were visible in any of our pictures even though (as in the picture here) BC approached to within seven feet of the camera in water that was crystal clear in any fishing sense. The reason why no legs show is, we believe, one of the by-products of the curious optical effect of "the sloping mirror" discussed in the text.

Above: Why the horizontal cast should be preferred to the vertical. In this photograph, taken when the anglers were seven yards distant, the horizontal rod is almost invisible, while the vertical rod looms into the window of the trout. The vertical rod always appears to thicken, when viewed through the window.

Private lives

Left: a magical moment – the mirror, the window, and a tiny nymph struggling upwards, urged onwards by some elemental drive towards its destiny in the sunlight.

JUST ANOTHER RIVERSIDE MIRACLE

Above: One of the most extraordinary dramas of the trout stream . . . as one female Baetis spinner crawls up from the water (top left of the photograph), another crawls down into it, to lay her eggs. We have timed these tiny flies on their underwater expeditions, and it is not uncommon for them to spend 30 and 35 minutes below the surface, only for some of them to re-emerge unharmed, their poetic act completed. But how do they survive so long, without air? They don't . . .

. . . the female takes her air down with her. As the fly enters the water (above, right) she folds her wings over her back, and (left) encapsulates a bubble, perfectly sealed along her back. It is enough for her to survive on, until her task is done.

The fly-fisher is a fortunate man indeed. A million private miracles like this, surround him every minute of his day on the river or lake.

Top...and bottom

How does the trout see flies in the dusk, when the angler cannot see them at all? These spinners, drifting over the camera like silent, eerie moonships, provide the answer. Although the fly may be invisible from above water, the last rays of light are refracted down from around its body and make it clearly visible when viewed from below water, against the sombre background of the mirror. Some refraction occurs while even the merest amount of light remains. The significance of this, when fishing in red sunsets, is discussed in the text.

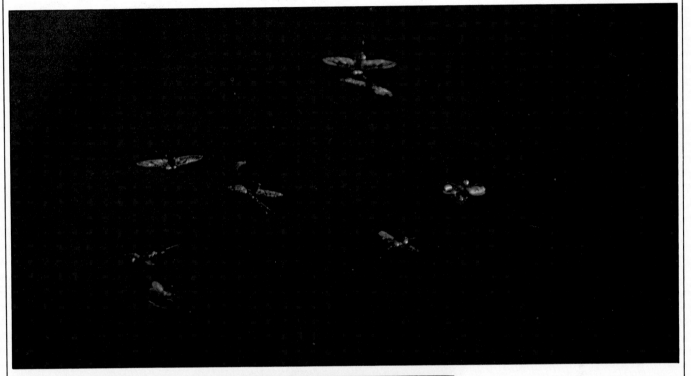

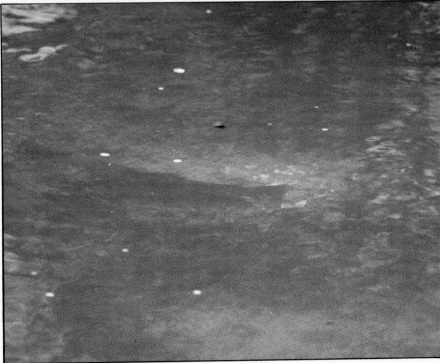

One of the most remarkable observations we have made is the way that large trout on some rivers clean or disturb small areas of river bed as a result of constant contact with their bodies, and the steady sweeping of their tails. This photograph clearly illustrates the points we make regarding this phenomenon, elsewhere in the text.

A range of new dressings

A fly-dresser's portrait, showing the key features of the USD Dun.

A fly-dresser's portrait, showing the key features of the USD Poly-Spinner.

A fly-dresser's portrait, showing the new-style winging of the Black Gnat.

USD Para-Olive

Suspender Nymph

Mayfly Suspender Nymph

USD Black Gnat (*top*) and
Suspender Hatching Midge Pupa

Caenis Spinner

Hatching Sedge Pupa

Mating Shrimps

G & H Sedge

Gerroff

PVC Nymphs

USD Hawthorn

Sunken Spinner

Grey Fox Variant

PB Mayfly

Super Grizzly

USD Mayfly Spinner

The acid test

How they compare: the conventional dun (left), the natural dun, and the USD Dun.

Left: The spinner in the mirror. In the centre, the natural fly; left the conventional imitation; right, our new dressing, almost indistinguishable from Nature's model.

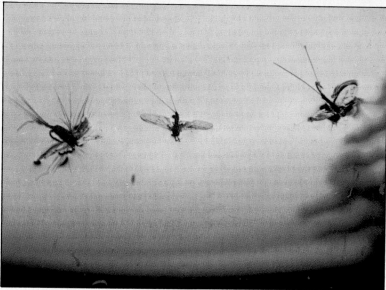

Below: The same three flies – and the same story – when viewed in the window . . . and note how starkly the hackles of the conventional dressing show up, when seen in silhouette.

Food for thought

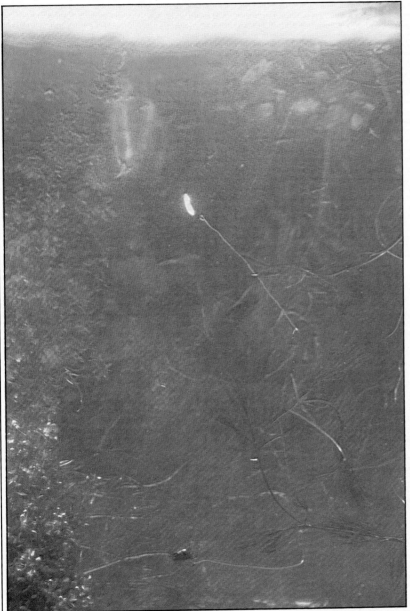

Left: A photograph of great interest to the stillwater fisherman. In the centre-bottom is an artificial nymph. In the centre-top, a blob of white light glows in the mirror. What is the connection? The blob of light in the mirror is the reflection of a strip of silver we built into the back of the nymph. The reflection provides an unmistakable focus of attention for any trout using the mirror to help it find food – and could do so even if the nymph itself were lost in the weed, and was impossible to perceive by direct sight. We discuss the implications of how the trout may use the reflective properties of the mirror to enable it to see around corners, more fully in the text. (The "line" in the picture is simply a length of wire which we used to hold the nymph still while we took the photograph.)

Right: Postscript – The proof of the pudding: a trout deduced by its behaviour (see picture, page 81) to be taking shrimp, and thrown to with the matching artificial.

A leviathan falls

A small, heavily-weeded trout stream that is never stocked . . . and BC sees a wild brown tight in to the bank. It rises to take a small dark fly. It looks huge . . .

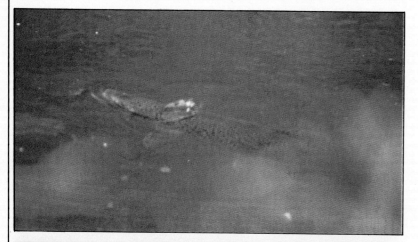

More rises come, and are studied closely. Eventually BC decides upon a suitable artificial . . . ➡

The moment of decision . . . an adjustment of the fins, a tilt to the surface, and the huge mouth opens in a confident take.

Deceived! The leader tightens, and the camera freezes the instant of Truth. Note the alarm in the fish's eye. What is it? What is it? What is it? ➡

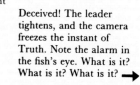

. . . and a battle of instinct versus skill amid the weedbeds. ➡

. . . and casts . . .

The fly alights and drifts over the big trout's nose. Time stands still and years of experience go into the assessment . . . Is that fly REAL?

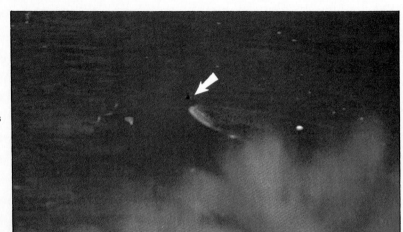

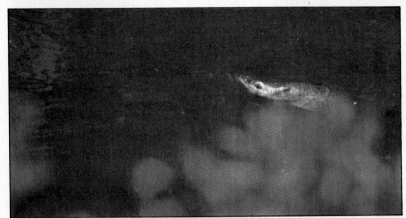

Panic, a wild lunge for sanctuary . . .

All over. BC with his quarry safely on the bank . . .

. . . and the story in a single frame . . . the trout, the hands, the leader, and the black feathered Judas clicked in his jaw . . . 3lb 14oz, the biggest fish off the stream for many years.

8 What the trout sees of the angler

In addition to our observations of the fly as perceived from below water we also, using a range of specially constructed observation tanks, and cameras sunk into the river bed, carried out a series of underwater experiments designed to throw practical light on matters of day-to-day consequence to the fly-fisher. The tanks we used were set up to reproduce natural underwater conditions found in the wild including (most important of all for observation and photographic purposes) *natural intensities of light*. The cameras we sank into the river bed were mounted in wholly natural stretches of water, unadulterated in any way. We will address our experiments and observations one by one; and where we believe it permissible we will draw conclusions from the results.

Visibility of the angler

Notwithstanding the theoretical position concerning underwater illumination (it is that a proportion of even the very lowest rays of light go down to the eye of the trout, with that proportion getting less and less as the rays get nearer the horizontal), we wanted to discover what the practical effect is on the angler of this fall-off in penetration.

To test the true effect, we constructed a pole 6 ft in height, with cross-pieces; and painted it with different colours of fluorescent paint (for visibility) at measured intervals down its face. We then positioned this somewhat gaudy "angler" at water level, at various distances from the edge of the window as perceived by an observer below water level.

As our "angler" was moved further and further away from the observer, a note was made of the lowest point on him which retained a meaningful shape. The angle between that lowest point, and the plane of the water surface, was then measured at each movement, with a theodolite.

At once, we made an important discovery. Although, thanks to the unnatural intensity of the colours with which the pole had been painted, we could actually see a trace of the lower part of the pole to a height corresponding to an angle of 1.9 degrees from the water surface, this trace visibility was of no practical use. The lowest light rays were so dull, so sharply refracted, and so compressed on the outside of the window (a point illustrated in Figs. 25 and 26) that nothing sensible could actually be *seen*.

It was only at an angle of 9.8 degrees to the water surface that parts of the angler became reasonably visible. It is for this reason that in our diagrams concerning the angle of penetration of light, and in our discussion surrounding them, that we discounted rays entering the water at less than 10 degrees to the horizontal. We are fully aware that some penetration *does* occur below that level, but this is of little practical value to the trout under normal circumstances.

From a typical surface feeding position of 12 inches below the film, the practical effect of a 10-degree angle was that the angler was clearly visible from a little below the waist up – and then, of course, very much foreshortened – at a distance of five yards. At 10 yards, only the head and top of his shoulders could clearly be seen.

There is, however, one important proviso that we would add to all of this. Any sudden movement below 10 degrees by a bright object could be seen at almost every point down the angler's "body" – even down as far as the 1.9 degree line, below which all vision was lost.

This finding clearly has some significance in the approach to the trout. While the trout is unlikely to see anything below the level of the angler's knees even when he is close up, it *does* argue even for careful movement of the hands, when working against a dark background in conditions of bright sun and flat calm.

The river angler is unlikely to find many fly-fishing stretches where the water surface is truly flat. The stillwater trout fisherman is, however – particularly on the smaller, man-made lakes.

The rod and clothing

We conducted a number of tests using gloss-varnished and matt-varnished rods in conditions of bright sunlight, at different distances from the window. In every case, when a gloss-varnished rod (particularly a flat-sided split-cane rod) caught the sunlight, it heliographed its presence to the observer below water, almost regardless of its position (Fig. 34). This, of course, was very much what we had expected to find, when taken in conjunction with our discoveries concerning movement set out in the paragraphs above.

It seems to us to provide a strong argument for the abandonment of the current practice of gloss-varnishing rods, and for matt-varnishing them, instead. There can be no knowing how many fish are not caught not because they have been "spooked", but simply because they have been put "on guard" by something as simple as the flash from a highly-varnished rod, even when it is being carried low-down by the angler. In all of our experiments concerning the reflecting powers of rods, the matt-varnished rod was much less easily seen.

In addition to the matter of reflection, we tested the visibility of rods at different angles to the surface, at different distances from the observer.

When held vertically, close to the traditional casting position, even the thinnest rod at 5 yards distant became grossly thickened by the effects of refraction: indeed, a 7 ft 6 in wand at 5 yards distant took on the appearance of a thick billiard cue, when held vertically. A similar – though less-obtrusive – thickening occurred when the rod was 10 yards distant.

In both cases, we found that the rod became less and less visible as it was dropped from the vertical to the horizontal; and that once below 45 degrees from the vertical, it all but disappeared.

This seems to us to provide the clearest case for preferring the horizontal cast to the vertical cast, even though in many circumstances it can be difficult to perform. This must be of particular importance when wading in broad shallows, and when fishing the open margins of rivers and lakes.

As a last test of the visibility of the angler and his accoutrements, we viewed

Fig. 34 Rod flash seen from below water. How many fish are put on guard by this, even before the angler's fly alights?

anglers dressed in a variety of colours, against a typical range of fishing backgrounds. As we expected, the clothing which best matched the background was the one that was the least visible from below water. The most visible colours, regardless of where they were positioned, were red, orange and yellow.

Flylines

One of the most vexed questions about angling equipment is that concerning the best colour of flyline for use in surface fishing. We decided to examine this subject in some detail, in an attempt to discover the truth.

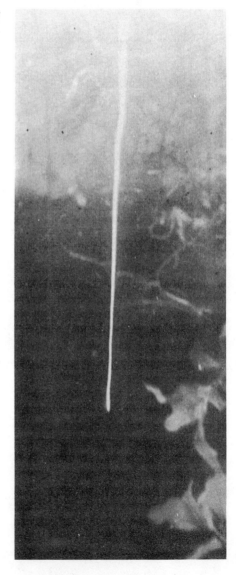

Fig. 35 What colour fly-line? Not a light one when the trout are feeding near the surface! (And note the colour photograph, page 86.)

All the debate that we have seen on this issue has concerned the colour of flylines both in the air and on the water, in the window of the fish. We therefore set up experiments that would allow us to observe white, brown and green lines, in each of these positions.

In the first instance, we cast the three lines at various distances *above* the water surface, across the window. At every level, the green and brown lines were more visible than the white flyline against the sky above. Towards the outside edge of the window, where there was a background of trees, the white line showed up marginally more clearly. In both cases, however, the white flyline showed one tendency that the others did not: in bright sunlight it gave off an occasional flash that was clearly visible below water. In the air, therefore, it seemed that the balance between the lines was finely placed, with the white line probably having the edge.

On the water in the window, the argument that the white flyline would be less visible to the trout when viewed against the light of the sky above, was proved fallacious. The white flyline *cut off* the light reaching the observer's position below water quite as effectively as the green and brown lines; and reflected light from the bottom, while slightly illuminating the underside of the white flyline, did not make any difference of practical account. Once again, therefore, we came to the conclusion that there was little to choose between the colours.

Then we decided to conduct a different experiment: an experiment to explore a point not yet raised in the public debate, and going beyond the visibility of the line in the air, and the line on the water, in the window.

We tested the three lines in the mirror.

The results of this experiment produced one of the most startling moments that we have experienced in the years in which we have been carrying out our research for this book.

We viewed the brown, green and white flylines lying in the mirror, when it was reflecting a bottom of (a) gravel and rocks, (b) weed, and (c) chalk-and-weed.

In every case, the white flyline was vastly more visible than either the green or brown flylines. It lay like a great bright crack in the face of the mirror; and when cast onto the mirror, it fell like a flash of white lightning across the whole field of view (Fig. 35, and see colour photograph, page 86).

It was quite clear from this experiment that a white, yellow or peach flyline can be a significant handicap on rivers, even when the angler knows where his fish is: he may be able to keep the bright line away from his target trout – but he is likely to spook more violently any unseen fish in the vicinity of the line where it falls on the water. And those unseen fish, when spooked, are likely to disturb the trout that he wants.

All this is even more important to the angler fishing still waters, however, than it is to the angler fishing in shallow streams for trout that he can see or pinpoint by rise-form. The stillwater angler rarely knows the exact position of his trout; and more usually casts without knowing how many fish are within his casting range, or where they are.

For the stillwater angler, it seems certain that the flash of white lightning across most of the surface field of view of any trout in the vicinity will startle or put on guard his quarry, and so will much reduce his chances of success. The only alleviating factor that can be employed by the man who uses light fly-lines on stillwaters in calm conditions, is a very long leader: it will enable him to put a greater distance between his fly or nymph and the "area of shock". In other words it will allow him partly to offset the disadvantage he has given himself.

We say this notwithstanding the fact that we have both used light-coloured lines (although, let us add, almost always in conjunction with long leaders) on still water hitherto. The fact is that, as a consequence of our experiments, we now know better their disadvantages.

We have also shown that any discussion of flylines against the light, whether in the air or on the surface, is largely irrelevant. It is the *mirror* that counts, every time.

Leaders

We tested three leaders of equal diameter, one greased with a flotant, one treated to sink by applying to it a compound of glycerine and Fuller's Earth, and one not treated with anything, but simply wiped clean with a soft, dry cloth. The greased leader came off worst in both the window and the mirror. Refraction around the edges of the flotant made it appear to "thicken" over and above the added width of the flotant itself. The leader that was simply wiped clean was fairly conspicuous in the surface film at every point, but was less easily seen below the surface. The leader treated to sink was, because of its opaque dressing, more easy to see below the surface than the wiped leader but, of course, it had the advantage of not appearing on the surface at all. In view of this, and the results of our drag observations recorded below, we had reinforced our faith in a leader treated to sink throughout the last few feet of its length, where fishing conditions and technique allow.

Drag

It is easy to understand, once it has been seen from the position of the trout, why drag can kill the angler's chances dead.

In addition to observing the appearance of stationary leaders in the mirror and the window, we observed leaders being drawn across the surface at different speeds.

We found that drag creates enormous visual disturbance when viewed from below; and that, perhaps not surprisingly, the degree of disturbance was proportional to the rate of movement. Anything other than the very slowest rates of retrieve set up a continuing series of thin fishbone ripples in the surface film, either side of the leader. Against the light, these fishbone crinkles flashed alternately light and dark, with the most pronounced visual effect occurring exactly where the angler would not wish it – on the edge of the window.

In each of these tests, the leader treated to float created worse drag than the leader that had simply been wiped clean. Again, the lesson seemed obvious; keep grease away from your fly – *particularly* when fishing dry.

Sunset and the dry fly

Various experiments that we conducted to discover how the appearance of a given fly might vary as the sun moved on its course during the day, resulted in one absorbing observation made with the spinner, at sunset.

BC had long believed that the effectiveness of the Orange Quill and similarly-coloured dry flies depended largely upon their position in relation to the sun, when perceived by the trout. In particular, he believed that the reason they succeeded *when* they succeeded (in the evening) was because the low red rays of the setting sun reflected off the wings of the natural fly, down to the trout below: in other words, that sunlight on the wings of the fly, changed the fly's colour.

He had already observed that the wings of the natural spinner, when held in a position to reflect the light, acted very much like cats' eyes at night. The cross-work of veins broke up the brilliance of the spinner's wings into a great number of highly-reflective facets – and the rays of the setting sun on these facets changed the colour of the wings to a variety of shades between pale pink and bright orange.

It was in setting up an experiment to test this theory under water that our surprise observation was made.

First of all, we found the theory concerning the upright wings to be partly proven: they did indeed take on a pink glow when viewed in the window from below water, when at an appropriate angle to the sun. The glow was not, however, as strong as we had expected that it would be.

Far more interesting was a phenomenon we had not even suspected – the effect of light from the red setting sun on the feet dimples of the dun *when seen in the mirror*; and its effect on the *spread-eagled wings* of the spinner, when similarly viewed.

In the case of the feet, instead of making a few sparkles of light like white diamonds, the indentations in the surface film took on the appearance of brilliant rubies against the sombre background of the mirror at dusk.

In the case of the spent spinner, the fly was utterly transformed.

The wings of the spent spinner always trap air beneath the corrugated patchwork of veins mentioned above; and the appearance of this trapped air in the mirror, under conditions of normal daylight, is rather like a piece of veined bathroom window surrounded by a white halo.

In a red sunset, when viewed from certain positions below water, all of this white light glows gold or red: the fly appears to glow like soft fire (see photograph, page 89).

Herein, we believe, lies one of the answers to the age-old problem of the difficult evening rise. It seems likely that as the light gets worse, the trout eats those flies he can most easily see – and science has already established that the colour the trout sees most easily in fresh water is . . . *red.*

If this is indeed the case it seems probable that when there is a colourful sunset, a fly with an orange hackle will attract the attention of many more trout than will an accurate representation of the natural fly as the angler sees it.

Our observation concerning the effect of evening light on spinners' wings and duns' feet in the mirror was made as the draft of this book was going to press. As a consequence, we have not had the opportunity to test our conclusion under field conditions. Nevertheless, we confidently expect a positive response from the fish, when we do.

BC watches intently as his fly comes back over a fish

A cloistered reach of a summer's stream, framed
by blossom and boughs

PART THREE

Technique

Man versus trout

9 Fishing the nymph

It is only in comparatively recent times that imitative nymph fishing has become a commonplace on clear-water streams – and upon the limestone and chalk rivers of England, in particular. And even then, the frontiers have been pushed back only slowly, in response to cramping definitions of what nymph fishing is – or *should be*, according to the man behind the rule-book.

Many definitions of nymph fishing have attempted to restrict the technique to imitations of specific kinds of insects (the *Ephemeroptera*), of specific sizes (small), fished at specific depths (in, or not too far from, the surface film).

In our view, all of this is nonsense. We do *not* believe that nymph fishing should be limited to specific kinds of insects, much less to specific kinds of fly. We do not believe that the size of the artificial should be limited by anything other than the size of the insect it is tied to represent. We do not believe that the depth at which a nymph is fished should be dictated by any factor other than the depth of the trout to which it is cast.

On the other hand, we *do* believe that the nymph should be fished selectively, to specific fish that can either be seen in the water, or that by means of water displacement betray the certainty of their presence at particular places in the water. We are as concerned as was any purist going back to Halford himself not to spook unseen fish, not to injure or alarm undersized fish, and not to spoil the chances of the man coming up behind, by casting at random about the river.

For the purposes of most of what is to follow, therefore, we write within a definition that accommodates the sensible safeguards, yet which nevertheless is neither unduly constraining nor prejudiced. It is almost a definition of fly-fishing itself. It is: "The casting to a specific, sizeable fish, of an artificial representation of the insect food upon which it is either feeding below the surface, or can reasonably be expected to be feeding upon, below the surface."

As will be seen in due course, there are circumstances in which we are prepared to move outside that definition. But they are circumstances, still, in which specific sizeable fish can be angled for; that spoil no-one's chances; and that call upon skill and wit to succeed.

The definition we quote is, for example, one which among other things does not prohibit the casting of the nymph *downstream* where the rules allow such an excursion – a point which our American friends will find it curious that we need to make; yet that will have the Puritans scurrying to early and willing graves.

But why on earth should a nymph *not* be cast downstream to a specific, sighted fish, when the upstream cast simply will not do: for example, to a fish lying upstream of an overhanging bush, or of a bridge support? Exactly the same arguments of principle apply here, as apply to the dry fly when fished downstream. To impose constraints upon oneself that either prohibit fishing at all, or that are quite absurdly limiting, is not only ridiculous, but the cause of much bad fishing.

Fishing – artful, skilful fishing – is about precision and delicacy. If a rule is imposed upon a water that prohibits a tidy and compact throw to a specific, impossibly placed fish and leaves open only the speculative or flukey throw, if one can throw at all, then that is silly. The flukey throw, the one-in-a-hundred chance of coming off, by definition does not come off 99 per cent of the time. And too often, the result is a frightened fish. That (and we are not asking for *easier* fishing – simply more sensible fishing) is a self-evident example of a bad rule, when a skilful downstream throw would do the job.

(Before moving a sentence further, let us qualify this statement. We fully appreciate that there are some club waters – particularly those with a very large membership – where a nymph cast downstream even to a specific, impossibly-placed fish, could lead to abuse. Where there is a heavy rod pressure from a group of anglers who do not know one another – or where there is doubt whether the code of sportsmanship will be followed by *all* rods – then there is no place for the downstream nymph. The interests of the fishery as a whole *must* come first, even if that means penalizing a responsible few. But the point we *want* to make is that there is nothing wrong or unsporting about downstream fishing *per se* – where it is used to a specific sizeable fish, with skill and accuracy. There is no doubt that many waters live under a wholly nonsensical blanket ban, handed down over the decades from purist forebears.)

In addition to the downstream throw, there are other things – equally fundamental – that our definition of nymph fishing does not prohibit: the use, for example, of nymph, shrimp and larvae patterns of quite unconventional *weight*: patterns which enable the angler to reach fish lying deep, deep down in fast-moving water; patterns that traditional nymphs normally dressed on sizes 16, 14 and 12 hooks could never reach. And our definition does not debar us from unconventional means of *presenting* such weighted nymphs, either. But before embarking upon all of that, let us look at conventional nymph fishing, briefly.

Traditional nymphing techniques

All trout take more of their food from below the surface of the water than from upon it; and it is for this reason that the ability to fish the nymph is such an important weapon in the angler's armoury.

Two important developments have sought to capitalize upon the trout's preoccupation with sub-surface food, in England. The first, of course, was brought about by the originality of Skues; the second, by the perception of that other great man, Frank Sawyer.

The contribution of Skues is already well documented. It was, quite simply, the conscious imitation of natural nymphs on anglers' hooks: the imitation as near as can be contrived from furs and feathers, tinsels and silk. The near-as-can-be nymph as developed by Skues (Fig. 36) is cast upstream of a sighted, feeding fish, and allowed to drift back to the fish, at its depth. Typically, the Skues fish is feeding close to the surface and weighting is not, therefore, incorporated in the dressing.

The technique that Sawyer developed is built upon Skues' pioneering work.

Fig. 36 The imitative nymph, pioneered by Skues.

First of all, Sawyer came to the conclusion that near-exact imitation was unnecessary. What Sawyer felt *was* necessary was a pattern that suggested the *appearance* of a natural nymph; and a means of presentation that suggested the *movement* of a natural nymph.

With regard to appearance, Sawyer's pattern is typical of all those developed by him: patterns which exhibit practicality and economy, above all else. Unlike the nymphs tied by Skues, the nymphs developed by Sawyer dispensed with the niceties. Sawyer, for example, did not incorporate a suggestion of legs in his most famous creation – the Pheasant Tail Nymph (Fig. 37). He concluded that legs were not necessary because his means of presentation was going to suggest the swimming nymph – and when the natural is swimming, its legs are not extended in the manner a hackle would suggest. Instead, Sawyer concentrated – insofar as physical *appearance* was concerned – on profile and colour to the exclusion of almost all else. What is more, Sawyer incorporated weight in the dressing so that it would penetrate the surface quickly, and would sink at least some way down to address a fish lying further from the surface (although not all that much further) than Skues' fish.

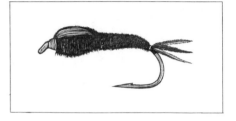

Fig. 37 Sawyer's Pheasant Tail Nymph—perhaps the simplest and deadliest nymph dressing ever developed.

But it was in the manner of presentation that Sawyer made perhaps his most dramatic contribution. His technique of the "induced take" as it is now called, wrests the initiative from the fish in a way that the method devised by Skues never did.

This is how the induced take is practised. A trout is sighted, and a weighted nymph of anything up to size 12 is cast upstream, ahead of the fish. Once the nymph has begun to drift back, and has reached a position just in front of the trout and marginally beneath it in depth, the rod point is raised. The nymph, of course, responds by rising up through the water past the nose of the trout, and the fish grabs it in a purely reflexive kind of way. Its predatory instincts have been triggered on the instant. It has been "induced" to take a fly which it might otherwise have ignored.

As an angling technique, the induced take occupies one of the pinnacles of artistry achieved in our sport. In terms of the demands which it makes upon the angler it is in our belief second only to the "deep nymph" as discussed later in this chapter.

Because it is so precise, and so clinically effective when performed well, the induced take has all but displaced the purely imitative technique of Skues. Certainly, the exactly imitative nymph can be important when the hatching nymph is being removed from the surface film, and when the ascending nymph is being intercepted just below it. But for most sub-surface fishing, there are very few occasions when Sawyer's spartan creation, when supplemented by one or two other dressings (such as JG's acclaimed PVC nymph, which is a specific imitation of the pale olive nymphs) will not do; and when Sawyer's induced take does not administer such medicines supremely well.

(There is just one point here, that we would add. Not even the Pheasant Tail Nymph needs to be moved, to succeed. Our first throws to a trout are always fished dead-drift; and only if the fish then fails to respond, do we employ inducement.)

None of the foregoing is intended to suggest that the upstream techniques of Skues and Sawyer are the only specifics for nymphing fish in alkaline streams. Numerous means have been developed, in the United States and Britain, for catching trout in rivers on the nymph. But there is only one other that we would mention here as a means of taking precisely observed, feeding fish. It is the very converse of Sawyer: the specific *downstream* throw.

In the United States, the specific downstream throw is known as the Leisenring Lift, a title which embodies both the name of its originator in that part of the world, and the action imparted. In the United Kingdom, it is a similar ploy to that which is not canonized by a title, but that is practised "blind" by many an expert wet-fly man, when addressing likely lies.

In fishing the Leisenring Lift (Fig. 38) the fish or lie is marked and the angler manoeuvres himself into a position from which he can throw down and across (or directly across) the stream to it. A hackled nymph carrying sufficient weight to sink quickly to the depth of the fish in the water is cast to land some way upstream of the trout, on a line that will bring it round in front of the fish. When the nymph is in front of the trout, and a foot or so upstream of it, the rod is lifted. The line tightens, and the nymph rises up through the water away from the fish. As with Sawyer's induced take, the response if it is going to come (and it comes very often) is immediate.

As will be apparent, there are direct parallels between this means of fishing the downstream nymph, and the technique described elsewhere in this volume, for inducing trout with the downstream dry fly.

But so to the substance of the matter.

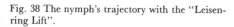

Fig. 38 The nymph's trajectory with the "Leisenring Lift".

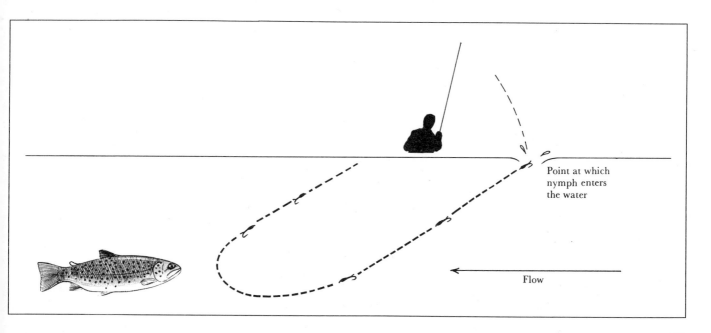

Point at which nymph enters the water

Flow

CONSIDERATIONS IN FISHING THE NYMPH

If there is one message that we would like to emerge from this volume, it is the paramount importance of observation in the business of successful angling. And of all the observation that the skilled fisherman employs, the most sensitive and the most intense is that which he devotes to his quarry before he casts. It is this observation that produces the clues which answer his most basic questions: *What* should I cast? *Where* should I cast it? *How* should I cast it? *When* should I strike?

Let us look at these win-or-lose questions now.

The pattern: weight versus depth

One of the reasons that nymph fishing is in the main so much more demanding than dry fly fishing is that whereas the dry fly needs only to be presented in two dimensions, the nymph must be presented in three.

Both techniques require judgments on length and breadth. Nymph fishing in addition requires a judgment on *depth*. And it is depth, when compounded by variations in the speed of currents, that presents the nymph fisher with his most formidable problem: how can a nymph be cast in such a way as to arrive at the depth of the trout in the water, by the time it has drifted back to the fish, from the point to which it was cast?

To help him to solve this problem, the nymph fisherman must employ two things in addition to his mechanical skills: the first, much the most important and certainly the most overlooked by the river fisherman, is *weight in his fly*; the second is an appropriate leader.

The question of the leader is discussed in some detail, a little later (see "The Deep Nymph"). The only observation that needs to be made on it at this stage is that in most instances an "appropriate" leader will be between 8 and 12 feet long, depending upon the nature of the water surface (for example, is it smooth or is it rippled?) and upon where the fish is lying (is it close to the surface, or 3 feet down in briskly flowing water?).

Care in judging the depth of the fish and the speed of the current – and the length of leader that is dictated by them – are of paramount importance because of a particular foible of the trout.

That foible is this. In our experience, *unless a trout is feeding avidly, and is taking pretty well everything that the current brings him, he is unlikely to rise up in the water to take something drifting over his head.*

This may seem a minor observation to make. But its importance to the nymph fisherman cannot be overstated. Unless his fly arrives at the depth of the fish in the water, above almost all else, it will be ignored by the majority of trout. The *great* majority of trout.

And the question of weight, which largely governs the sinking rate of the fly, becomes critical. This is true *regardless* of the depth of the water being fished when the trout he is after is not snapping up every morsel of food. *It can be as true for a fish lying in 18 inches of water, as it is true for a fish lying in several feet of water.*

110

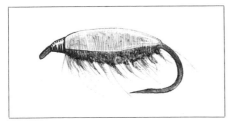

Fig. 39 The artificial shrimp.

What patterns capable of carrying weight, then, does the well-armed nymph fisherman need?

For a fish lying in a slow current at depths of 2 and even 3 feet or less, the Pheasant Tail Nymph in sizes 16, 14 or 12, will not only be appropriate in size, but in weight.

Where the current is brisk or turbulent, or where a fish is lying deeper down, then more weight will be needed than a Pheasant Tail Nymph of natural size, can embody. In these circumstances the artificial shrimp (Fig. 39) comes into its own.

The shrimp (*Gammarus*) lends itself to the carrying of weight in an artificial design because it is a comparatively stout creature for its length. In practice, a shrimp can be dressed on a size 12 or 10 hook and still look natural, even with 8, 10, 15 and even more turns of lead wire under the dressing.

The shrimp we most often use is a simple affair constructed of seal's furs and clear PVC or polythene, and is shown in the diagram.

Presentation: the importance of invisible currents

In fishing the nymph one of the factors that can make the difference between success and failure is the ability to capitalize on any hints that the fish might give on where the cast should be made. And as ever, it is close observation that reveals the clues.

For example, because the general flow of the current is in a downstream direction, it is a mistake to believe that the fish always lie facing upstream. Individual fish do not lie in general currents. They lie in individual sub-currents that very often indeed are not in a true downstream direction.

Sub-currents are created when the general downstream progression of the water is checked or diverted by features of the banks and the bed, and by vegetation growing from them. They can vary from minor deflections of the water from a true upstream–downstream course, to the full-blooded back-current found at the edges of hatch-pools, weir-pools and the like. And any fish lying in such a current will be facing at a slight angle in the case of the minor deflection, and due downstream in the case of a back-eddy. And of course, it can be facing at any angle in between, just as the water can be moving at any angle in between.

This factor can be of crucial importance for the angler's line of attack. All it needs for the fisherman to fail is for his cast to be made due upstream into the general flow of the water, instead of due upstream into the *specific* flow of the water in which the fish is lying. In the latter case, the nymph will arrive from the direction in which the fish is looking and from which it is expecting its food to appear: in the former case, it will not.

How is the angler to know into which sub-current his cast should be made, or his nymph be guided? It will be revealed by the attitude of the trout in the water (Fig. 40).

In the figure, the current has in one case been divided by a gravel bed, and in another case deflected by a fallen tree. It is quite probable that a cast to

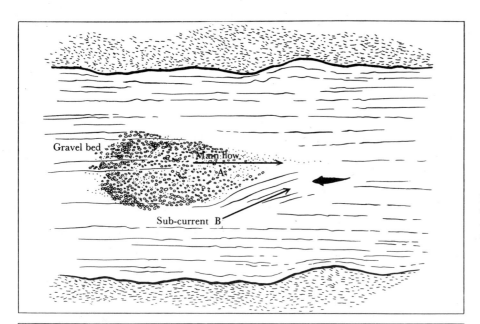

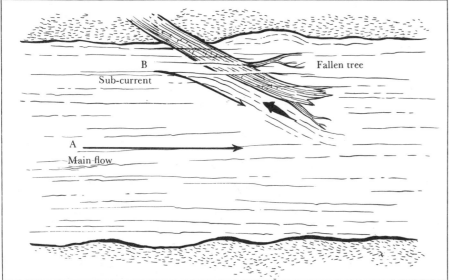

Fig. 40 The attitude of the fish in the water reveals the direction from which it expects its food to arrive. In these diagrams, the correct cast is to "B" even though the main current is coming from "A".

point A would be useless in each case, even though the cast would take the fly very close to the fish concerned.

The reason is simple enough. Each trout is interested in food being borne to it by the sub-current in which it is lying. That, indeed, is why in all probability it is lying there. So it is concentrating its attention in the direction of B. A successful cast to each of these fish will need to be directed at B, as the attitude of the fish makes plain to the observant angler.

It is not, of course, simply gravel beds and fallen trees that divide and deflect the current. Dense weedbeds, piling, camp sheathing, sandbanks, sandbags, formations of rock, potholes and many other features of the typical stream exert their influence upon the flow of the water, and upon the fish which must face directly into it, to survive. The trout is adept at deciding which flukes in the current will bring him most food. Watch him carefully, and he will unwittingly reveal his decision to you.

Do not only watch *him*, however. In planning your attack on a particularly desirable fish, watch the rapturous behaviour of the weed below the surface. Follow the progress of natural flies *upon* the surface. Fix your eyes upon pieces of detritus lilting and tumbling along the bottom, where the water is sufficiently clear. All give the most precise clues to the strength, nature and

112

direction of the flow – and invaluable help in deciding where the cast should be made.

Tactics: (i) the deep nymph

In most rivers, quite large numbers of trout lead long, happy and unbludgeoned lives not because they are particularly wily, but because conventional fly-fishing techniques simply ensure their preservation.

On some rivers, these are the fish that lurk in deep, slow holes: fish which tend to be larger than the average, which rarely rise and which seek most of their food from the bottom or close to it. On others – the limestone rivers and the chalk streams, which for reasons of their own seem less well endowed with such still, silent places – there also live fish which remain untouched by the conventional nymphing techniques (the Sawyer and Skues techniques) used against them.

In the case of these fish, it is because they lie in and feed in slower flukes of fast current, far down in hatch pools and weir pools, and in other swift-flowing water of between five feet and 10 ft deep – and even more (Fig. 41). And the *reason* that they remain supremely unmoving (and unmoved!) is because the conventional artificial nymph passes far over their heads.

Fig. 41 A hatchpool. When fish are feeding on nymphs and shrimps several feet down in water like this, the only answer is the deep nymph—the most demanding of all fly-fishing techniques.

Some of these fish *can* be caught. Not all of them, by any means – but some of them.

Because of the depth at which they lie and the surface turbulence one often finds in swift-flowing water, it is only a small minority of such deep-lying fish that one sees in the first place. And quite often, because of that perverse and special law which anglers trail behind them wherever they go, even all the fish that can be seen cannot be fished for, because of the nature of their lies and the bankside vegetation. But that still leaves *some* – and of these, let us say again, some can be caught.

Those that are caught, are well caught. They are hard-earned fish that the vast majority of fishermen would pass by even if they chanced to see them. They are fish that leave a summer landscape in the mind and a warmth, like old port, deep inside.

The technique that we have developed to catch them, we have christened "The Deep Nymph". It is the most difficult of all the forms of fly-fishing that we know.

What is the deep nymph? It is a technique which emerged when we first began to look at the problems posed by deep-lying fish, and tried to establish the requirements of any technique that would be capable of success against them. We will go through our thought-process here.

The overriding requirement in addressing a fish lying deep down, we decided with numbing brilliance, was to present it with a fly that it could actually see. And in view of the deep, fast nature of the water, that meant regarding whatever pattern we ultimately used *as a vehicle for weight,* first and foremost. It was – having regard to the fish's reluctance to rise up in the water to take a fly – the same principle we discussed earlier in this chapter, though expressed in a more extreme form.

The second requirement (because fly-fishing is an imitative art) was to provide the fish with a fly that still looked like food, notwithstanding the amount of lead it had to carry. A third requirement was that the fish should be undeterred by the manner of presentation; a fourth, that we should have a good chance of knowing when the fly had been taken; and a fifth (because the most likely fly to be taken by a fish is that which goes nearest to it) was that the fish should have to make little or no effort in accepting the hook.

If the first and most obvious requirements were that the fish should not only see the fly, but see it as food, then for the reasons concerning sinking rates that we discussed earlier the Pheasant Tail Nymph was out of its depth, and our good friend the shrimp, in its element. Though not this time our comforting and familiar shrimp, but a shrimp regarded first and foremost as a vehicle for weight: a shrimp designed to carry sufficient lead for it to sink to the depths in the fastest of water, and advertise its place on the menu.

To meet this requirement, we have when addressing trout in deep, heavy, turbulent water used shrimps dressed on wide-gape size 8s, carrying anything up to 20 and more turns of lead wire around the shank.

The problem of casting such a heavy pattern – and what is more, casting it with a high degree of accuracy – was where the difficulties began. But before it

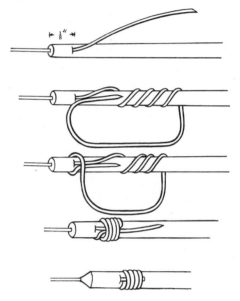

Fig. 42 The needle knot.

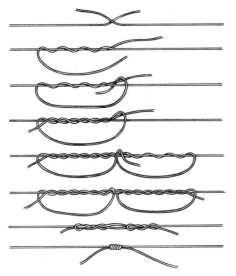

Fig. 43 The double Grinner knot.

could be cast, it had to be attached to a leader. But what *kind* of leader?

The first thing that became apparent was that the conventional length of leader was worse than useless, for several reasons. One was that the plummeting shrimp would quickly sink the available nylon, and would then begin to sink the flyline itself – and the water resistance of the relatively bulky flyline would drastically reduce the rate at which the nymph would go down. In other words, it would in part negate the effectiveness of the lead built into the fly.

A second (though lesser) problem was that there was a risk of the line being dragged down to such a depth that it would alarm the trout below: that it would "line it" subaqueously, as it were. This might be less of a problem with a dark flyline – but it could be real enough with the white, yellow or peach-coloured lines so popular with many anglers.

A third consideration was that the subtlety of the leader to which one looked to record the vital take would be replaced by the coarseness of the flyline itself as the register. (While in practice many of the takes were to turn out to be savage affairs, with the trout having to make a now-or-never lunge to something desirable speeding by in fast water, we knew from experience that any take which needed to be seen to be hit would be more readily observed on a heavily greased floating butt than on the end of a flyline way under water.)

In overcoming these problems, we ended up using a leader of similar length and design to those we often use when fishing the nymph on still water: as short as necessary, but in practice anything up to 14 ft, 16 ft and 18 ft long: leaders of a staggering length, so it was to transpire, to those who fished rivers in a more traditional, less searching manner.

While in a purely literal sense it is virtually impossible to avoid "lining" the fish (because the fish is lying deep, and the nymph has therefore to be chucked a long way upstream of its position), nylon is a great deal less obtrusive than thick flyline – and we have rarely seen a fish disturbed by it. What is more, the fine diameter of nylon offers little resistance to the sinking shrimp, and so assists its sinking speed. Further, greased nylon will float on the surface where it can be seen; and as a consequence, we are enabled to retain all the sensitivity that we have in detecting the take on a conventional leader, should we need it.

It is a simple matter to construct this unusual and versatile leader. A couple of feet of 22 lb–26 lb nylon are permanently needle-knotted to the end of the flyline (Fig. 42). Using the Grinner Knot (Fig. 43) – a knot that is far stronger than the blood knot – next attach the last six or seven feet of a 9 ft knotless tapered 7 lb b.s. leader from which you have cut the heavy butt; next, add 18 inches or so of 6 lb level monofilament, also using the Grinner Knot; and lastly, using the Grinner again, add as many feet as you need of 5 lb level point material.

This is a simple leader to make up: far removed from the multi-piece nonsenses that have been foisted upon us all by the angling press for years; a simple leader of enormous length, and yet one containing *only three knots*. A leader that, given reasonable conditions, will turn over (nay – be *dragged* over!) nine times out of ten, by the weight of the nymph at the end, when cast.

It is no easy matter to present accurately, in three dimensions, an extremely heavy shrimp on the end of a very long leader; but it can be done, and done consistently. Of course, one must be sensible. It cannot be thrown into a strong breeze; it cannot be cast amid dense vegetation or where a high fence is crowding up from behind. But given a reasonable position and an absence of wind or a gentle breeze from behind, the cast can be made and fish can be taken.

Here is how to present a deep nymph.

First of all, gauge the depth of the fish and the speed of the current. Pick a shrimp of suitable weight having regard to these; and decide how long your leader will need to be, according this time to the depth of the fish, the speed of the current, and the weight of the nymph you have chosen. In fixing the length of the leader, remember that it will not sink in a straight line to the bottom, but in a generous curve; and remember, too, that you will want the two or three feet of the butt at least, to float and register the take.

Finally, decide where you will need to cast the nymph, for it to be brought back to the trout on its line *and at its depth*. In other words, go through exactly the same thought processes as you would in addressing a less-deep trout with a conventional leader – but make amendments of scale.

The cast (for the right-handed angler) is made as follows. With the rod in the right hand, hold the shrimp between the finger and thumb of the left hand and then gradually pull off line from the reel with the fingers of the left hand that are free. Waft the rod from side to side in front of you, so that the line your left hand is pulling from the reel is worked out through the rod rings. The leader and some line will soon form a wide, airborne arc in front of you, from the shrimp in one hand to the rod in the other. The moment you judge there is sufficient flyline in the air to flex the rod, let go of the shrimp. *Immediately* go into a normal casting rhythm, and the line will work out in the usual way. The shrimp and the leader will perform wondrous feats in the air beside you, but they will not tangle.

When sufficient line is airborne to deliver the shrimp to the spot you have chosen, let it go in the normal way. As soon as the line begins to unfurl in front of you, gently slow its progress as it speeds through the controlling fingers of your left hand, by applying gentle pressure with them. The line will slow down and straighten, but the heavily-weighted shrimp will continue its journey, and carry the leader out behind it. It will all straighten neatly, to your absolute astonishment.

Once the shrimp has been delivered, fish the cast out in the normal way. As we have mentioned elsewhere, however – do not expect a typically gentle take, if the water is heavy as well as deep. The take can sometimes be savage. More than once, we have had rods almost wrenched from our hands by fish lying deep in fast water.

In concluding the deep nymph, we would emphasize that we only use leaders of such extreme length, under the circumstances described. A leader of

116

great length has no place under ordinary conditions, for fish feeding close to the surface on rivers.

Tactics: (ii) drawing fish from cover

One of the most useful tactics that we know in the whole field of nymph fishing is the drawing of fish from cover with what we have termed elsewhere as the "plop!" delivery: a cast that is contrived deliberately to drop the fly into the water close to the fish, with a controlled disturbance. The emphasis, we would add, is on the word "controlled". A disturbance as punctilious as a full-stop, though – if such a thing could be achieved – an energetic full-stop in which spray is thrown two inches or so into the air.

The "plop!" delivery is achieved by abruptly retarding the shooting of the line, just as the leader is turning over. Stopping the "shoot" by grasping the line in the fingers of the left hand (for the right-hander) enables the momentum of the shrimp to carry the leader sharply over, and causes the fly to dive down into the water surface.

We first discovered the effectiveness of this delivery when fishing on still waters. It works, we believe, because it *commands* the attention of the fish. The "plop!" sets up vibrations in the water, which the fish feels. What is more, it creates an explosion of light sparkles as it cuts through the mirror, and an ebbing of rings that the fish would need to be blindfolded not to see.

This combination of stimuli – vibrations, movement, and light-patterns – proves far too much for the rainbow trout, and quite enough for many browns. It has nothing at all, we believe, to do with any Pavlovian reactions on the part of stew-bred fish that have subliminal recollections of scattering pellets. We have used the "plop!" on wild trout in Ireland, Scotland, the West Country and the North with results that have been just as consistent: on fish, that is to say, that have never seen a pellet.

As we have confirmed with such fish, the "plop!" is a wonderfully effective way of taking the mountain to Mohammed: of bringing an apparently inaccessible fish from the safety of its cover into open water. Time after time we have caught fish that were seemingly invulnerable, by using this tactic. Two classical examples of its use are for the fish that is feeding beneath the overhanging branches of a tree, and for the trout that lies beneath a bridge.

A typical situation is shown in Fig. 44. (Typical, that is, for us: the other man's typical fish always rise midstream, at places where there is a clear backcast that can be floated up into a gently following breeze which turns the leader over beautifully. *Our* typical fish rise beneath dense thorn bushes under far-distant banks; just the far side of electrified fences; a little upstream in the field with the bull in it!).

The fish in Fig. 44 is lying in a wholly inaccessible place, close into the bank, screened by a veil of willow fronds. You can hear him rising, you can see him rising, but you cannot get a fly to his position beneath the tree.

Put up a size 12 or 10 shrimp with a little weight in it, and cast just off the willow fronds, as closely as you can to the trout. At the very last moment, as we

Fig. 44 The most common circumstance in which the "plop!" delivery proves its value—in drawing an otherwise inaccessible fish from its cover under a tree. The trout is rising at A. A weighted shrimp delivered with a distinct "plop!" will cause the trout to break off from its feeding under cover, to hunt down (and probably take) the fly at the centre of the disturbance, at B.

have just described, retard the shooting of the line to cause the shrimp to carry ahead of the leader, and go in with a tiny disturbance.

It is remarkable how often the same pattern of events ensues. The fish, if it was due to rise, does not. Often, there will be a surge on the water surface as he moves out or drops back rapidly, to investigate. There is a pause for a moment or two and then the leader stabs away as he picks the shrimp up and moves back to his position.

Exactly the same tactic can be used against the fish beneath the bridge (Fig. 45). He looks invulnerable, and to the conventional approach he probably *is* invulnerable.

But the shrimp that plops in just behind him will extract him as smoothly as a winkle on a pin. The fly goes in, he turns to hunt it down, and takes it. Just, as the saying goes, like that. It is a clean, efficient *tidy* way of fishing. There is no nonsense about trying to squeeze a cast into an obviously impossible space between the water and the underside of the bridge – scaring, as such efforts so often do, the fish out of his ichthyological wits. Nor is there the throw across

Fig. 45 The fish lying under a bridge is another candidate for the shrimp delivered with a "plop!" into the open water behind him.

the width of the bridge, in hope of the fly curling down onto the water, and drifting down to the fish, drag-free.

Again, this is not to suggest that we want to remove *challenge* from fly-fishing – heaven forbid, we do not. We are concerned to *increase* challenge in our fishing; and for that reason more than any other, are more interested in difficult fish, than in fish we know would succumb most easily.

What we *are* concerned to see go, is thoughtless and cavalier fishing. Occasionally it is amusing to try for a near-impossible trout here or there – but almost always it leads to untidy fishing that results in the fish being put down when the fly is retrieved from its snag on the planking; or in the fish breaking away around an arch, should the fly chance to fall aright.

No fish that will probably break away should be thrown to in the first place. It is bad fishing, irresponsible fishing, *inhumane* fishing. And if the angler doesn't want to use something like the "plop!" – which itself calls for wit and skill to execute well – then he's better not trying at all for the trout we've just discussed.

Tactics: (iii) the sunken spinner

For some years now it has been known that the female spinner of the Medium Olive (*Baetis vernus*) crawls underwater to oviposit, and it has been suspected that other species of upwinged flies may follow the same procedure. Both Frank Sawyer and the late Oliver Kite mentioned this fact in their books, but since then no new facts have come to light, and certainly to our knowledge no one has ever suggested fishing a weighted spinner pattern to represent the egg-laying female underwater, as a regular tactic. However, thanks to recent work in this field, we now have an interesting and often productive new tactic open to us.

Before describing the procedure in detail, let us take a brief look at the behaviour of these egg-laying females. We have now established conclusively that the following species oviposit underwater: the Medium Olive (*Baetis vernus*); the Large Dark Olive (*Baetis rhodani*); the Small Dark Olive (*Baetis scambus*), and probably the Iron Blue (*Baetis niger*). There may, of course, be other species that oviposit in the same way, but at the time of writing those listed above are the only ones we have been able to identify with certainty.

When these female spinners are ready to lay their eggs, they fly out over the water looking for emergent vegetation, rocks, boulders, posts, piling and the like. They alight on these and quickly crawl underwater, looking for suitable egg-laying sites, usually found on adjacent weed (see colour photographs, page 88).

They will often travel several feet under water before selecting a site. Once they have laid their eggs, the spinners are usually too exhausted to climb back to the surface. They simply release their hold and float up to the surface film, beneath which they are carried along by the current in the "spent" condition.

These relatively tiny flies can remain underwater for long periods – as long as 30 minutes or even more – and it was only while taking the series of colour photographs showing these spinners actually crawling underwater that we discovered exactly how they achieved this feat. Under high magnification, these photographs clearly show extensive bubbles of air trapped beneath the wings, and in the hairs of the body. It is a reasonable assumption that in some way they are able to utilize this air during their underwater excursions.

These spinners, which oviposit in either the early mornings or evenings, are an attractive target for trout, which quickly learn where the egg-laying sites are situated. At the appropriate time they take up station a yard or two downstream and feed on the spent spinners as they float towards the surface. In some situations – where posts, rocks or the brickwork and piers of bridges are chosen by the spinners – the trout can be seen actively engaged in picking them off the wood or stonework as they crawl down. Under bridges, the trout so engaged are often among the largest to be found in the river; and those that regularly feed in this manner can be recognized by their white lips – the wear, of course, being caused by constant contact with the rough stonework. In the past, it was generally thought that trout feeding in this manner were picking the green moss or algae off the brickwork.

The weighted pattern developed to represent these spinners (see the section on fly dressings) is a most effective and lifelike artificial, and is dressed in several sizes to match whichever species of spinner may be on the water. It should be fished in exactly the same manner as one would fish a normal weighted nymph, although it seems to be most effective when lifted towards the surface, in a manner which simulates the rapid rise of the buoyant natural spinner. The lift, of course, induces a take from the trout in the time-honoured way.

In addition to the above, this new pattern has a further, valuable use: it is an excellent alternative to show an experienced fish that is feeding on hatching nymphs. If the fish refuses your artificial nymph, try it with this new spinner pattern. You may be pleasantly surprised at how readily it accepts the novelty. Towards the end of the season, after most of the trout have been concussed by conventional weighted nymphs (and there is no doubt that they come to recognize many of the more common nymph patterns), they will often accept this new dressing with confidence, even though there are no natural spinners in the water at the time.

Tactics: (iv) some minor diversions

There are two other tactics that every nymph fisherman should have up his sleeve.

On hard-fished waters, where the trout have seen the induced take many times before, they will often hold back from a fly that is conveniently twitched in front of their noses. But if we cannot offer them an induced take with success, how can we attract attention to a fly drifting inert amid a mass of natural food? The answer is – "lock the fish on", early (Fig. 46). Cast upstream of the fish, and allow the fly to drift back into its field of vision. When you're confident that the fish can see your fly (though from some way off) lift the rod-end to attract attention to the nymph. *Then let everything come back in dead drift.* The movement will often be sufficient to focus the attention of

Fig. 46 On some waters, the fish so often see the "induced take" that they either ignore it, or else it positively alarms them. But that does not mean they cannot be caught by inducement. Cast well above the trout, A; allow the fly to sink well down and then, when it is still several feet in front of the fish, draw the line to give the fly a distinct twitch, B. If then allowed to travel dead-drift to the fish, C, it will quite often be taken in preference to natural nymphs.

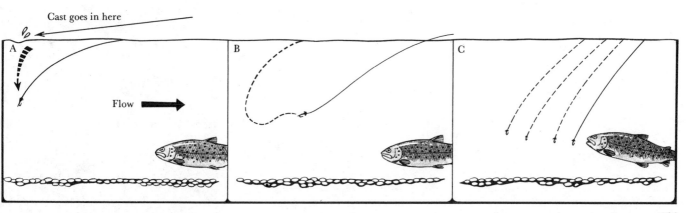

Cast goes in here

A

Flow

B

C

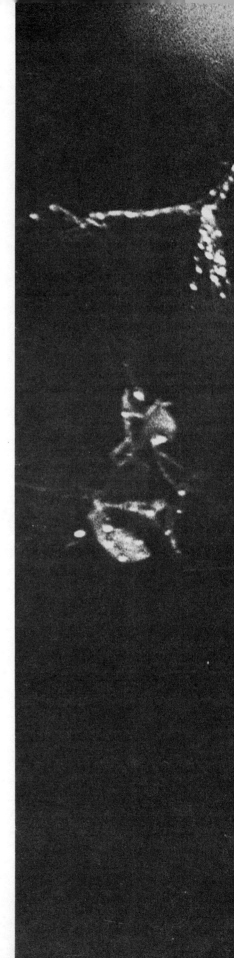

a trout otherwise suspicious of the induced take, on an inert creature it sees drifting helplessly towards it. Sometimes the result is a take, where a refusal might have been expected.

The second minor tactic is the use of the "plop!" in slow water. It is a technique we developed in the great drought of 1976, when the rivers shrank back from their normally full flow to become trickles interspersed with pools. It was in these pools that the larger fish took up residence; and often enough so slack was the flow that they could be observed treating these pools almost as still waters, swimming restlessly around in circles.

The problem here was to give the fish a long enough sighting of the fly in shallow water, before the fly sank to the bottom. It was overcome by dressing a shrimp-like creature short on the hook, without any additional weight. The material we used was the same seal's fur used for our standard shrimps, but we dressed it fluffily to entrap significant amounts of air.

The result was a fly of sufficient *bulk* to create a "plop!" and attract the attention of the fish; but that sank very slowly, giving the trout plenty of time to see it. So effective did this pattern become, that BC christened it the "Gerroff!" – a truncation of his call when, time after time, smaller fish would appear from nowhere to grab it, when he had cast to a bigger fish on which his attention had been focussed.

What a happy angler's world it would be, were the problems always thus!

A death in the morning, caught in a spider's snare

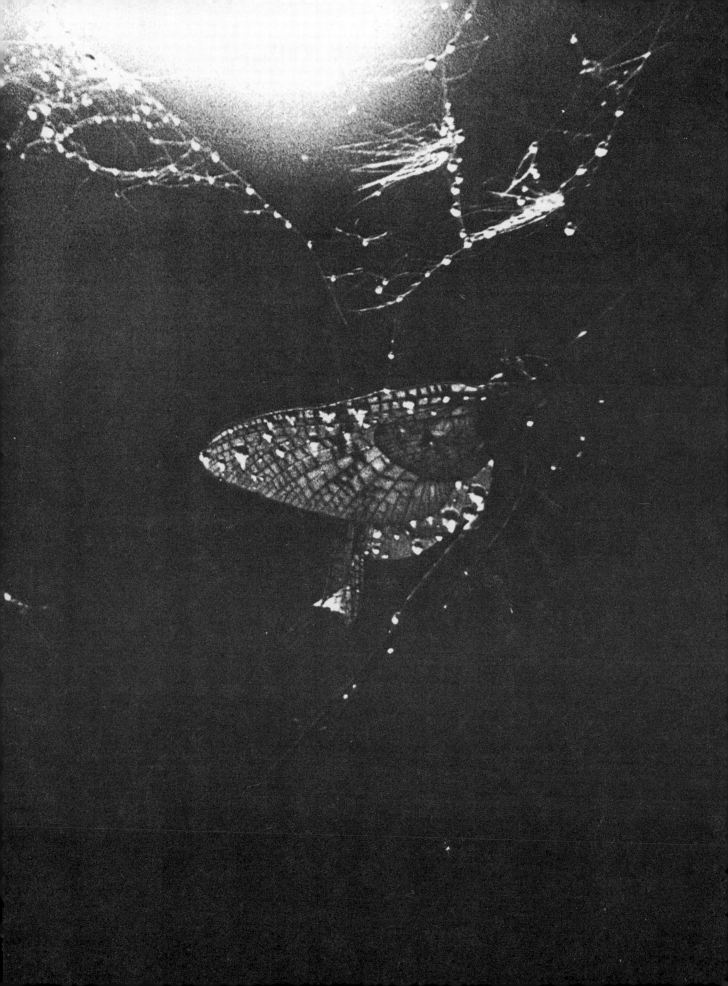

10 Reading the take to the nymph

We have, in the chapter on the nymph, expressed our view that nymph-fishing is a more demanding branch of fly-fishing than is the art of the dry fly. And we stated there that one of the most obvious differences between the techniques is that nymph-fishing must be practised in three dimensions instead of two.

There is a second, equally obvious and no less important difference between the arts. It is that the dry fly man is rarely in doubt when his fly has been taken: one moment it is there, gliding down upon the surface film with all the dignity it can muster; the next moment there is a splash, sip or roll at the surface, and it has gone – persuaded elsewhere by a fish that in all probability has been seen as well.

How different it all is with the nymph. Not only can the nymph man only rarely see his fly, but the fish does not break the surface for him at the moment of the take. Often, indeed, the fish takes well below the surface in a patch of reflected light that conceals him from the angler completely.

So it is for this reason, too, that nymph-fishing is so much more difficult than dry-fly fishing: because of the difficulty of knowing when the fly has been absorbed. And to be sure, all is academic if the fly is taken, and the angler knows nothing about it.

What the nymph fisherman must do, therefore, is to ally *concentration* to his powers of observation. The nymph fisherman simply cannot afford to be more-or-less aware; to "see" things in some passive kind of sense, as though through a window. He must *watch* – actively, alertly, almost aggressively, for clues that his offering has been canonized with acceptance.

The things that he must watch for are the fish, the water it swims in and the leader that he delivers to them both, for signs that the trout has taken. Exactly where he applies his greatest concentration depends upon whether the fish he is casting for can be seen at the moment of the take or not.

The take and the visible fish

The golden message in nymph-fishing, if the trout itself can be seen, is – watch it. Forget the water. Forget the leader. Forget everything but what the fish itself is doing.

And if the right nymph is cast to the fish on its line, and sufficiently far upstream for the fly to arrive back at the depth of the trout in the water, what should we be expecting to see the fish do? Let us look at each of the most common occurrences when nymph and fish coincide.

The whitening mouth

The old advice to the infantryman – "don't shoot till you can see the whites of their eyes" – can be freely adapted by the fisher of the nymph – "strike when you see the white of his mouth".

To anyone unaccustomed to fishing the upstream nymph, the idea that the fish can be seen to open and close its mouth when it takes may sound like an observation from a distant planet. But the fact is that the mouth of a feeding fish can clearly be seen granted reasonable water and light, because as the mouth opens it gleams with an unmistakable whiteness (see photograph, page 81).

The whiteness only shows, of course, if the fish turns towards you as it takes; or if the fish is lying opposite you on the current. But if you have cast to the fish, and your nymph is anywhere in the vicinity when the fish opens its mouth, then tighten. Tighten even if you believe your nymph to be some distance removed from the fish when the fish opens its mouth: it is astonishing how often, given the perversions of the laws of refraction and the sneaky things that sub-currents can do with a fly on a leader below the surface, that the nymph is *not* exactly where you could swear that it is.

So tighten first, and regret later. But *only* tighten. Do not wrench the rod hard back – particularly if the fish is going in the opposite direction. A brisk raising of the rod-tip, only a little more positive than if you were feeling for the fish on the end of your line, is all that is necessary. This is particularly true if (as we hope is the case) you are using barbless hooks.

By describing it so, we do not mean that you take things casually. Do not, for example, wait for the fish to *close* its mouth, having once opened it. Your fish will not be deceived long, and the process of sucking in a fly and spitting it out again, can be achieved in a twinkling. When your fish has his mouth open, he has the nymph inside. Either he has engulfed it by swimming over and enveloping it, or the very act of opening has sucked in the water in which the nymph resides.

It is in this respect that the strike or tightening to the nymph, is utterly unlike the strike to the dry fly. It is easy to strike too quickly with the dry fly: it is almost impossible to strike too quickly with the nymph. If you do not yet do it – and it is something many fly-fishermen do automatically – you can almost double the speed of your strike by bringing the non-rod arm into play. As the take occurs, raise the rod and simultaneously pull in line with the free hand. The effect is that the time taken to pick up a given length of line is much reduced.

Other takes of the visible fish

If the visible whitening of the mouth is the most reliable clue that a fish has taken the nymph, it is by no means the *only* clue that the average fish affords.

If the fish you are casting to *lifts* in the water when your nymph is near it, you have a further warning of when to tighten (Fig. 47).

A fish only lifts in the water if it is a feeding fish anxious to investigate or intercept something drifting over its head. It takes at the upper limit of its lift, while it is still at an angle to the surface. It has whatever it is going to have in its mouth at the moment it begins to level off, or turn back down. So prepare to tighten as it lifts, and raise the rod as your quarry straightens out whether or not you have seen its mouth open.

If your cast is not absolutely true for line – and usually, unless you walk

125

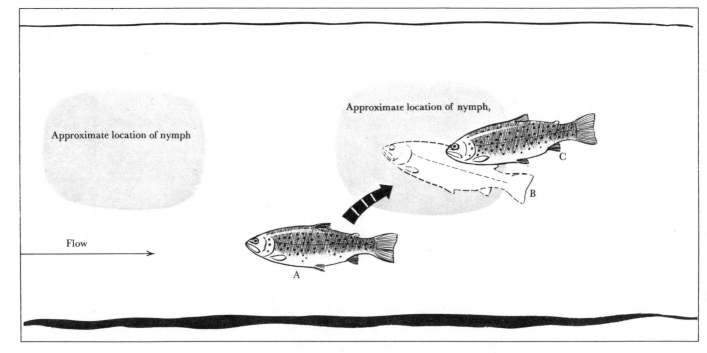

Approximate location of nymph

Approximate location of nymph,

Flow

A

B

C

upon the water and lower your fly in, it will be a few inches to one side – the fish will have to move *horizontally* to take. The horizontal movement is a more positive diversion than the lift just described. The lift, as we have said, is little more than an adjustment of the fins; the horizontal movement of the fish turning to intercept something passing it by in the current, is achieved by a positive thrust of its body.

If the thrust is towards you, you may well see the certain clue of its mouth blinking white. If you do not see the mouth open, tighten as the fish turns to regain its lie. If the thrust of the fish is away from you, again tighten as it turns back to its lie. Sometimes, it's worth noting, a fish will move so far to either side to collect a nymph that you will be as surprised as he is when the connection is made.

There is one last point that we would make, before leaving the takes of the visible fish. It is this: do not be in too much of a hurry to lift your nymph from the water, once it has passed the fish by. For reasons best known to itself, a trout will often allow a fly – particularly a big one – to travel some way behind it, before whirling like a demon possessed to grab it. Unless there is an obstruction on which your fly or line will snag, let your nymph travel several feet below the fish before lifting it clear of the water.

The take of the invisible fish

It is in fishing for trout that the angler cannot see at the moment of interception – usually because a visible fish has dropped back into an area of

Fig. 47 The lifting or "assumed" take. The trout is lying at A. It lifts in the water to B, somewhere in the region of your nymph, and immediately levels out (C) before returning to its lie. Strike the moment it begins to level off in the water. The fish will often have the nymph in its mouth at this point, even though no actual "take" has been seen.

reflected light in following the nymph down – that the nymph-fisherman comes closest, the non-angler will swear, to black magic; to knowing when the fly has been taken, even though neither the fly itself, nor the obliging fish, can be seen.

But there is, of course, no black magic in it. Success in fishing for a trout that we know is there, but cannot see from the casting position, depends upon knowing what we can expect the fish to do; and in understanding what the water will do in reacting to the movement of the fish, and what the leader will do in reacting to the fish, as it takes the fly into in its mouth.

As we saw in discussing rise-forms to the natural fly there is a direct relationship between the movement of the fish, and the movement of the water in which it swims. If the fish swims quickly to intercept a natural nymph, it will displace water violently. If it swims more slowly, it will displace water more gently. But as it is with the natural fly, so it is with the artificial. The water does not refuse to react to the movement of the fish simply because the fish has made the error of moving to intercept an artificial nymph in mistake for the natural. So the first things that the nymph-fisherman must learn to look for are displacements of the surface film: for sudden variations in an established surface flow; for changes in areas of reflected light; for contortions in reflections from the sky or the bank.

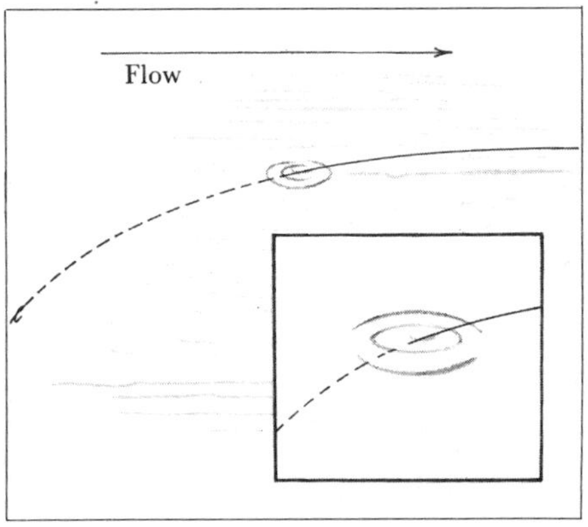

The second thing he studies in his search for clues, is the behaviour of his leader-point. And in particular the tiny "hole" that the leader-end seems to make, where it cuts through the surface film (Fig. 48). Because just as there is a connection between the movement of the water and the movement of the fish, so there is a connection – in the most obvious and literal sense – between any movement of the fly on the end of the leader (any movement of the fly in the mouth of a fish, on the end of the leader!) and the leader itself where it floats upon the surface.

In studying the leader on the surface film, the nymph-fisherman reacts to anything that is consistent with a pull on the end of the leader, or a slowing of the leader as it rides downstream on the current. Exactly how vigorously such events will be signalled depends in part upon the speed of the current. If the current is slow and sedate, the offer can be recorded with great subtlety if, indeed, it is recorded at all. If the current is brisk, then the leader will be moving at a similar pace, and anything that interferes with its progress will be more noticeable. What is more, if the current is speeding the fly downstream, any trout that wants to intercept it must grab it quickly, before it is swept away. So in fast water the current working on the leader and the fly, and the circumstances which the weight of water imposes upon the fish, militate against a subtle take. A high-speed fly intercepted by a high-speed fish is likely to make for a very obvious take indeed.

Some subtle takes

There are only two reasons why the leader-end moves, other than when the hook has snagged itself on some sub-surface obstacle. The first is because the

Fig. 48 Movements of the leader at the point where it enters the water, are a basic clue to unseen acceptances of the fly below the surface.

leader-point is dragged steadily down by the weight of the nymph; the second is because a fish has *pulled* it down, in taking the fly.

First of all, the downward movements of the leader under the weight of the nymph cannot be ignored. If the nymph is unweighted, the leader will tend to sink unevenly, in fits and starts. Little, other than when some wholly untypical fit or start occurs, can be learned from this. But if the nymph is well weighted, it will tend to draw the leader-point down smoothly and steadily at first, with the speed of descent gradually reducing as the natural buoyancy of the nylon begins to inhibit the nymph's downward plunge. Then, if the point of the leader stops sinking abruptly, when the fly is in the vicinity of the fish – tighten. Conversely, if the leader-point suddenly stabs down at an accelerated pace when the nymph is in the vicinity of the fish – then also tighten. These are two typical takes to the nymph. They are extremely difficult to detect; and there can be little doubt that many takes of this kind are not seen, even by the experienced angler.

Another subtle indication that the nymph-fisherman looks for is when his leader, which has been drifting back on the surface at the pace of the current, suddenly pauses or falters momentarily, and then continues its progress. Again, this is a very common take. There is no drawing down of the point, no movement to one side. There is nothing, save a pause so subtle that it might never have occurred.

This ability of fish to intercept flies so gently, was clearly demonstrated to us when we were carrying out experiments in water that was gin clear and very slow moving. We were not trying in these experiments to *catch* the trout: we were more interested in observing their reactions to a fly that JG had designed to sink very slowly in conditions of low-water, the bizarrely-named "Gerroff" (see page 172).

One of us watched the fish, the other watched the leader. Time after time we saw fish suck in the nymph and spit it out again, without moving the leader at all. At one point, BC saw a fish suck in the fly, chew it in a puzzled kind of way with its mouth opening and closing, opening and closing, and spit it out again three times without ever moving the leader on the surface.

For the nymph-fisherman on rivers, this is a revealing observation. It shows just how many times his fly might be accepted, without his leader having the courtesy to tell the tale. (And if it is a cautionary tale for the river fisherman, it is one to leave the nymph-fisherman on lakes with an empty feeling inside. Most of *his* takes occur when his nymph is sinking down through the water after the cast has been made – and goodness knows how many takes go unrecorded on still water, where there is no current to emphasize events.)

It is not, however, the case that takes to the nymph are always so difficult to see, even on slow moving water. The single most common form of take is a simple twitch of the leader end, to one side; or a pronounced stab downwards as mentioned a moment ago.

There is one further point that we would make concerning the trout's acceptance of the artificial fly, and it is this. All the variations in the take which we have discussed here are *in addition* to any other phenomena that might occur. And nothing at all is *felt*. The angler who fishes the upstream nymph, and who waits to feel a pull as in wet-fly fishing, is wasting his time. A pull will not be felt more than one take in some hundreds. The whole burden in successful nymph fishing falls upon the eyes, and upon the speed of reaction to what they see. And most of what they see will be unspectacular, indeed.

There are so many signs of a take to look for, that the newcomer to nymph-fishing might well believe that it is all beyond him. In practice, however, it's not as difficult as it sounds. The observant angler quickly comes to recognize an unusual movement on the part of a trout he is watching, and then a raising of the rod-tip becomes semi-automatic. Even with movements of the leader, which can be much more subtle, it is surprising how quickly natural reflexes take over.

A simple way of convincing yourself of this, if you have the opportunity of watching a nymph expert in action, is to ask him after he has caught a fish, how he knew that his fly had been taken. Quite often he will be unable to tell you. His mind will have become so finely attuned to the abnormal, that any of the clues described above will register automaticaly, and signal his arm to raise the rod-tip. Many times this has happened to each of us, when showing companions how to fish the nymph. We have simply not been able to say what it was that made us tighten.

But what it was *not*, was magic!

A silent place where the world stood still, close to the river's bank

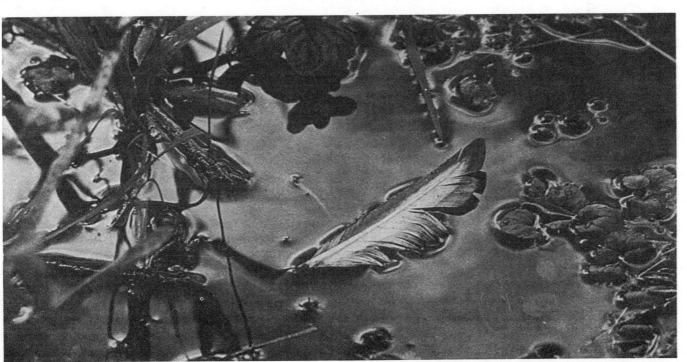

11 Fishing the dry fly

The literature of fly-fishing is a minefield of disagreement: sometimes disagreement on matters of profound importance; but more often dispute on issues of momentous inconsequence. One of the most sterile of all the debates is that which surrounds the question of imitation and presentation: more properly – because that is the form it has taken – the question of imitation *versus* presentation.

In the blue corner, there is the "exact imitator" (and what an exemplary inexactitude *that* is!); the man who claims that imitation is all, and who burdens himself with copies of every insect at every stage of its transient existence. Each fly in his box is waiting for that wondrous moment when it will constitute *exactly* the right dressing, of *exactly* the right size, with *precisely* the correct length of hackle, and the number of tails just so.

In the red corner, we have the pragmatic presentationist. Secreted somewhere on his person will be two small tins – one of them containing the ossified shreds of yesteryear's tobacco and half-a-dozen fag-end nymphs; the other containing among similar fossils a couple of carpet-fluff dries. It doesn't matter in the least about imitation, says the presentation man: it's the way that the fly is delivered to the fish, that matters.

Let us declare now that if it *were* a question of either/or, then the presentation man would have the greater edge, by a nautical mile. But it *isn't* a question of either/or. It is a question of both: of imitation *and* presentation. Sometimes, imitation alone will do the trick. Far more often, presentation alone will do the trick. But for consistent results with experienced fish, one must be able to deliver the correct fly in the correct way.

What exactly is the "correct way?" Better still, what exactly is "presentation" itself?

The classical, conventional way of presenting a dry fly involves the casting of the artificial dun or spinner a few feet upstream of the waiting fish, so that the fly can be drifted back over the trout, without movement. If the fly is a dun, then it is treated to float *on* the surface film. If the fly is a spinner, then it is presented flush with or *in* the surface film (and so it is at this earliest stage in the attack that an understanding of the rise-form and what it can reveal, is so valuable: it is of fundamental importance not only in the choice of fly, but in its presentation).

The basic mechanics of fishing the dry fly as specified above have been spelled out a thousand times in angling literature, and we do not see value added by repeating them here. Before moving on, however, to discussion of a dry fly technique that is in our view of profound importance (though at direct variance to the approach outlined above), there are a number of lesser considerations that we wish to address. They can have a significant effect upon the angler's bag.

The first concerns delivery of the fly to the water.

As we said a moment ago, the classical presentation of the dry fly is by means of a cast which delivers it upstream of the fish. One of the reasons it is delivered upstream is to give the trout a good sighting of it as the fly drifts back.

But there *are* times when one does not want the fish to have a good sighting of the fly. One such occasion is when a fish is so busy hoovering up the fruits of a heavy hatch of fly that to present the artificial as just another natural would give it very little chance of being picked out. Another instance is when it is clear we do not possess a tolerable likeness of the fly in demand. In each of these cases there is an excellent reason for not wanting to chuck well upstream of the fish, and give him time either to miss the fly in the first instance through sheer weight of numbers, or time to study and reject it, in the second. In each of these cases, there are things that can be done to increase the chance of success.

The first priority is to note the regularity of the fish's rise: familiarize yourself with his tilt to the surface, to the point where you can anticipate when and where his next rise is due. Then cast – but *directly upon the fish*, and not upstream of it, as in the conventional way. By this device, the fly will fit in with the fish's gastronomic clock, will arrive in the right place at the right time, but will not have been seen in advance, and will not have been appraised.

If that fails, then deliver the fly a few inches upstream of his nose, a split second after it has broken the surface for his regular treat. Sometimes the effect will be to induce him to break his regular rhythm, and to take immediately, a second time.

There is one other ploy that can be called upon when the fish is eating a fly we do not possess. It uses the rise-form itself to overcome as much of the disadvantage as possible. It is particularly helpful when the surface is glassy smooth, and the fish has a clear view of the flies overhead. The fish rises to the surface and sips, slashes, head-and-tails or rolls; he breaks the surface film and sends an ebbing of rings or wavelets about himself. Cast into the rings *immediately* – it is the one opportunity you have of presenting him with a distorted (though still fly-like) view of your artificial. Quite often his appetite will overcome his discrimination, and he will be persuaded to take the new arrival. Do not deny him the pleasure.

Self-selection by movement

One of the most interesting – and infuriating – trout that can be encountered is the regular riser that ignores the most precise imitation that fingers, thumbs and prayer can design, no matter how perfectly presented.

Up our tormentor comes – glug, sip, wallow; down he turns again. Then up – glug, sip, wallow, and away he glides once more. Rise-glug-down-pause; rise-glug-down-pause.

Watch the rise, and watch the natural fly he takes. It is one of the least-often observed but most important phenomena during a rise to surface fly, that individual naturals often select themselves for consumption. They become unwitting suicides, if we may coin the contradiction, because they attract attention to themselves.

Imagine the scene. The river is carpeted with flies; a silken conveyor-belt of food. Once every few seconds a fly over any given piece of water, moves. It flutters its wings to dry them after hatching, or it tries to take off and it fails. In doing so, it sends out a tremble of rings on the water-surface about it. The light shines through them and ebbs in winking rings of brilliance, down through the water below.

And the trout reacts. It does not think – it is not capable of thinking; and it does not look for something different, either. It is simply programmed with a finely-tuned predatory instinct; it is one of Nature's own in pruning out the weak, the lame and the foolish. Flutter-attract-food-bang! Flutter-attract-food-bang!

In this case, the traditional dead-drift, float-without-drag is a dead loss.

If the fish is selecting only flies that move, then *your* fly must move. Throw upstream of him, wait until the artificial is somewhere just behind his shoulder, and twitch the fly a couple of inches. Sometimes (though not always) the fish will turn and take – and with the utmost confidence, at that.

We are conscious that in the last few paragraphs of this chapter, we have said that "sometimes" the fish will take. And in a moment we are going to do it again. The fact is that there is no such thing as certainty in fishing. Yet the hallmark of the expert fisherman is consistency. It is *flexibility* which gives him that consistency. The flexible fisherman – the man who observes the natural order, reads its messages and adapts his technique to meet them, is the man who succeeds. *Not* because he has some infallible formula (other than concentration and attention to detail), but because he adds up the "sometimes"; because, through adaptability based upon observation, he can place himself in the path of a wide range of options; because he can see that sometimes this will work, and sometimes that, and sometimes the other. He multiplies his chances of success by perception and understanding. Unlike the man down the bank, he is not playing some kind of roulette. If he is not in charge of the table, then he's got money on most of the numbers.

The biased riser

There is another fish that we want to mention. He is some distance away, close to the far bank. You cast to him again and again without either frightening him, or putting him down. Or – more to the point – without rising him, either. Yet experience tells you you're doing everything right. You're almost certain you know what he's taking, and have got a reliable representation tied on. You're casting to his near-side, so that the leader doesn't go across him – and you know in any event that that's the safest thing to do: if you put the fly this side of him and he does turn, he'll have the fly facing him first, and not the leader-point.

Watch this fish with great care, and pose yourself two questions: (a) does he consistently rise to one side of his body (in this case the far side)?; and (b) does he tend to be a splashy riser? If the answer to either of these questions is "yes", drop as far behind him as you can, *and cast to his other eye.*

It is by no means uncommon for a fish to have defective sight; and it is quite common to find fish that are completely blind in one eye. We catch two or

Fig. 49 (Picture 1) Sometimes a trout will rise consistently to one side, and any fly that is cast to the other will be ignored. Here is the usual reason: a trout blind in one eye—its left in this case. (Picture 2) This photograph shows the right eye of the same fish. Note how the fly has clicked into its scissors as the fish turned left to regain its station.

three such fish apiece, in the course of a season (Fig. 49). It is obvious why a fish with only one good eye, should rise to the side on which he has sight. He is often a splashy riser because he has problems homing in on a fly by monocular vision – and any fly he sees overhead he is likely to see late, causing him to lunge for it, at the last moment.

The absent riser

So far, we have been concerned with the fish that is rising persistently. But not every fish, alas, is so accommodating. Quite often a fish will pause between rises – and refuse our artificial when it is offered, no matter how accurately cast to the rise-form.

The persistent throw to the rise-form when a fish is rising spasmodically is a common cause of failure. It is common, because we do not think carefully enough. After all, it seems such a reasonable thing to do. Why should one not cast to the rise-form, if that is obviously where the fly is being taken?

The reason why not, is a good one. *The fish is not there when your fly arrives.*

133

It is a common occurrence in water of any depth, to find a fish sighting his food in one position, and taking it in another position several feet, or even yards, downstream (Fig. 50).

What this fish is doing is lying in wait for food to come towards him. What is more, he is lying in some depth of smooth, sleek water. The water is not roaring by, to cause him to grab. The surface is not rumpled and bobbled to give him an uncertain target. He is lying well down in steady water, that gives him plenty of opportunity to see what is coming. When he sees something interesting on its way, he does not swim directly up to the fly: he is too concerned to save energy to do that. He simply adjusts his fins, and allows the current to drift him upwards *and downstream* on a trajectory that will cause him to intercept the object, at a point some distance behind his original position. His movement, as we have observed elsewhere, is very like that of a seagull riding the breeze.

Even if he decides to make an interception he will still be several feet behind his observation post, behind the position in which he lies in wait, behind the point at which he makes his decision on whether to ascend or not. But if he is a shy and experienced fish, he may *not* take the fly at the point of interception, but study it from close range. And as he studies, he drifts even further from his observation post.

The lesson, then, when fishing to occasional risers on sleek, deepish water, is to *begin* by casting to the rise-form; and then to work the throw upstream, delivering the fly a yard ahead, at a time. (Once in a while your fly may arrive on the fish's head, and put him down. But that will be a comparatively rare event – and you can always mark his position, and return later.) On deep water, do not give up on the fish until you have covered the water five or six yards upstream from the rise-form.

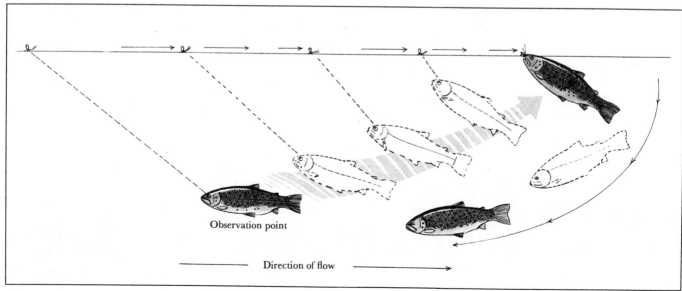

Observation point

Direction of flow

We cannot over-emphasize the importance of this. Many fly-fishers fail to catch trout that are rising and ready to be caught, because they simply do not show their flies to the fish. The tendency of the trout to drop back before taking – particularly of that most desirable fish, the big, experienced trout which characteristically lies over deep water – is one of the least-widely recognized phenomena in fish behaviour. At the same time it is one of the most common, and one of the most fundamental to success.

The downstream dry fly

On a river we often fish, there is a bend below an island. The water on both sides of the island is thrust into two powerful streams that cut deeply into the bank on either side of the river. All the food that the river carries is funnelled down into these two rumpling tongues of water. When there is a hatch of fly, these currents are like entomological soup, croutons and all.

On one side, on the left bank of the river looking upstream, there is a heavy shawl of woodland. It provides excellent cover for the fisherman.

The day had been a pleasant one on that stretch of the water: no lemming capitulations, but a fish here and a fish there, and a couple more besides. BC was in the middle of an excellent season: one in which the fish hunger had long since departed and he could now apply himself, with honour saved, to musings and experiment.

On the way back towards his car, as the gloom gathered about, he decided to experiment with one of the oldest methods of all – the dap. On the water, his small artificial sedge dribbled its way up the surface film. It was difficult to see but the thin, trickling V that it made in the current wrinkled and winked out behind.

Fig. 50 Trout do not rise vertically in the water to take surface flies—they drift back on the current to intercept them at a place some way downstream from their observation point. Sometimes the drop-back and scrutiny process can cover many yards. When it is completed, the fish will return to its original position, to await the next fly. Clearly, a cast to the rise-form under these circumstances will fall behind the disappearing trout.

Within a minute there was a splash, a wrench at the rod-top, and his arm was dragged viciously down. Somewhere in the dusk a heavy fish careered downstream before coming high out into the air in a distant white plume, and breaking free. Somewhat astonished, BC reeled in and checked that the fly was all right. It was, and as a matter of curiosity he put it out again, allowing it to dribble its way upstream as he inched his way slowly to the car. In the next ten minutes, several more fish attached themselves to the sedge; and the evening became the first of many experiments that we have conducted in attempting to suggest not only the appearance of the natural insect, but its movement.

Experiment with the moving dry fly is, of course, a hanging offence in some traditional circles. But the fact is that almost all living insects move in some way upon the surface of the water. Indeed, we described an example – when a fish was selecting only those flies which were obviously moving – a few paragraphs ago. Necessarily, on that occasion, the fly was cast upstream, and moved downstream. But that is by no means the most effective movement.

Of all the movements of a fly that the trout finds it difficult to resist, the *upstream* movement, against the current, is the one that attracts the most excited attention.

Exactly why this should be so, we do not know. Perhaps it is because the upstream movement of the fly creates greater resistance to the downstream movement of the surface film, and so exaggerates the light patterns seen from below. Perhaps it is because the fish is programmed, as part of Nature's population control mechanism, to react to the movement of egg-laying females. The females almost always move upstream when ovipositing, and many species dip their abdomens into the water, to deposit their cargo.

But whatever the reason the reaction is called forth, called forth it is. And it is a reaction that can be conjured to devastating effect, *by casting downstream*.

On a river where dry-fly purism blindly reigns, as we have just said, to suggest such a course would be to invite a grisly end – though why it should be so, we do not know. A fly, after all, can be cast just as selectively downstream as up. It can represent the appearance of a natural fly, just as well. It can suggest the appearance of a *living* natural fly far better. It does not spook any more unseen fish than the upstream fly; and with all of these criteria filled, it need spoil the sport of no-one. Additionally, it is more difficult to fish than the upstream dry fly – a point which, we should have thought, would have kept *everyone* happy.

There are only *two* good grounds, in our view, for banning the downstream dry fly. The first is where such a ban is the most desirable of a variety of options available for limiting the kill on a given stretch of river (and we know of many better ways, given conventional circumstances). The second reason – much more generally valid, we believe – is when downstream fishing is likely to be abused. As we discussed when writing of the nymph, there are undoubtedly some large associations where any chink in the rules will be exploited. Yet the rule against the downstream fly is almost universal on clear-water streams, and is applied with a blimpish mindlessness even on those waters where it *could* be practised.

There are two ways in which the downstream dry fly can be fished seriously.

The downstream twitch

The first and most effective method of fishing the downstream dry fly is one in which movement directly upstream is imparted to the artificial, just before it reaches the trout on its downstream journey on the current (Fig. 51).

This is how the downstream dry fly is fished. The instructions are described for a right-handed angler.

The river is flowing from right to left, and a trout is spotted that is taking surface fly some distance across. First of all, position yourself slightly upstream of the fish. With the rod to the right of your body, begin to aerialize what you judge to be sufficient line to deliver your fly three or four feet to the far side of the fish, and just upstream of it. Deliver the final punch to send the line on its way, and do one of two things designed to send the leader and the end of the line in a curve from right to left: *either* add more power than you normally would with the rod, *or* pull back the shooting line a little, at the last moment.

Fig. 51 The downstream twitch. A loose curve-cast (A) is made to a point a few feet above the trout. As the fly drifts down towards the fish, draw the line briefly, causing the fly to move an inch or two upstream (B). Let all immediately go slack again (C) and prepare for a savage take. (The cover illustration shows the "twitch" in action.)

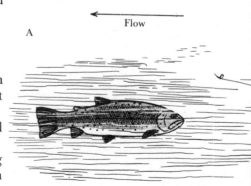

A

Flow

Given a reasonable wind and a great deal of practice (this is not an easy cast to make, and you will not get it right every time) the fly on the end of the leader will be carried round in a ragged, right-to-left curve. And if you judge it correctly, the extra few feet you shoot in the first place will be accommodated by the curve: the fly will land nicely upstream of the fish, and on his line.

(To achieve a curve-cast on a river flowing from left to right, make as though you were deliberately going to over-throw, and then impart less force, instead of more, as described in the previous cast. With practice, you will be able to judge it so that the momentum of the line is sufficient to achieve the distance required, and the leader will flutter limply to the water, downstream of it. Both of these casts are, of course, helped by a downstream wind.)

Whichever cast you have made, you have now got the line on the water, and the leader and fly downstream of it, pointing towards the fish. Allow the current to carry the fly towards the fish and then, when it's a couple of feet in front of the trout, raise the rod momentarily. The fly on the end of the leader will be twitched upstream. Once that movement – and we're talking only of a matter of inches – has been imparted, lower the rod to allow the fly to drift naturally again, *and steel your nerves*. The upstream inducement with the dry fly can be every bit as deadly as the conventional "induced take" of Sawyer, which moves the nymph downstream. Often, the fish will launch itself at the fly, like a missile. When he does, "give" him the fly by dropping the rod point – and then, after a brief pause, raise it firmly again. This procedure is important in fishing the dry fly downstream. Unless it is followed, the fish can be very difficult to hook firmly.

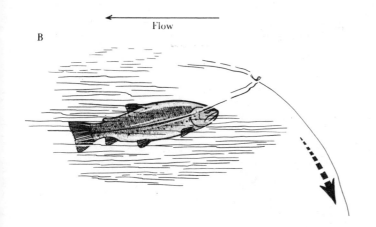

B

Flow

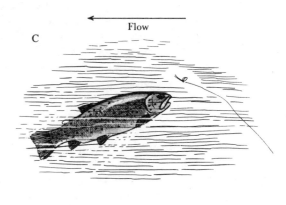

C

Flow

It is not always possible to fish the downstream twitch in the manner just described. Sometimes it is necessary – for example, if the fish is tight under your own bank – to fish directly down to him. Then, keep your rod as low as you can, and drop the fly in a straight line for the fish, but a couple of feet above him. Hold the fly back a fraction when you're sure he can see it, and then lower the rod as before. And again, "give" him the fly before tightening. A snatched strike will usually result either in a missed fish, or a pricked fish.

The downstream twitch works particularly well during the sedge hatch in the evening; but it is also very effective indeed when fished as described, during rises to the *Ephemeroptera*. Where allowed, of course, it is the perfect medicine for the fish that is feeding on self-selecting flies, as discussed earlier; and for the trout that cannot be covered from below.

The downstream dry fly, as we have said, is far more difficult than the upstream dry fly; but it does possess several advantages.

One of these is that *the fly gets to the fish before the leader*. The fish can, of course, see the leader if it can see the fly. As will be apparent from the chapters on fish vision, the trout could, if he looked, see the leader running across the surface of the mirror. But with the fly floating towards him, that is where his attention will be riveted. He can focus very accurately on the feet of the fly, and is unlikely to be aware of the leader that adjoins them.

With the conventional upstream throw the leader often cuts through the mirror and the window close by the trout the instant the fly alights on the water. And if the fish is going to be alarmed, it will be alarmed more quickly by a fly that arrives on the end of a leader slicing through the film beside it than it will be by a leader drifted towards it on the current, behind a fly on which it is already concentrating.

A second advantage that the downstream cast provides is that it enables fish to be reached that it would have been impossible to reach with the upstream throw. It gives us a second stratagem, for example, for the fish lying upstream of a bush in the water, or for our old friend above the bridge support (Fig. 52). And it can be used for those infuriating fish (and they are many) that lie above sills. The fish above the sill or weir is protected from the upstream throw because the fly, leader and line are immediately dragged downstream by the toppling water, where it disappears to the depths below. The downstream dry fly overcomes all of that.

But two words of caution: one concerning your approach; the second, your leader.

As will be clear from earlier chapters, the eyesight of the trout is acute. The trout has good binocular vision ahead of him and if you have to throw directly down to him, he will see you if you are careless. If he does not see you, he may see your rod waving above your head, unless adequate back-cover is available. Only a *long* and *horizontal* throw will overcome his advantages when addressed from an upstream position, on a bank that is devoid of cover.

The second word of caution concerns drag. After the fly has passed the fish, the fly will drag in every case on the downstream throw. And not only will the fly drag: the whole line and leader will drag as well, once the line has been

Fig. 52 Two obvious candidates for the downstream dry-fly, where the rules permit.

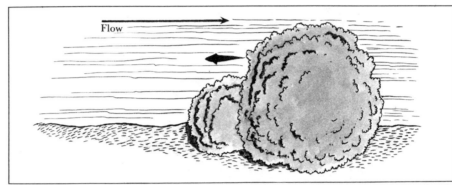

straightened out by the current. For this reason you will not get many chances when you have to cast directly downstream. If the first or second throws do not look exactly right from the start, retrieve the fly before it gets close to the trout, and cast again.

If the throw *is* right but the fly is not taken, wait until it has travelled some way behind the fish, flick it under the surface with a quick twitch of the rod, and manoeuvre it away to one side. To assist an inconspicuous recovery, it is a good plan to lengthen the leader if a cast has to be made directly downstream.

There is one last point: *avoid* the cast that has to go directly downstream, if you can. Wherever possible, always position yourself for a *diagonal* throw. It makes more demands on your casting, but is much less likely to spook the fish – particularly when the fly is being retrieved.

The downstream arc

Unlike the downstream twitch, the downstream arc is a minor tactic: but it can be very useful when trying to take fish under awkward circumstances – for example, when the cast must be made far down-and-across, or when the vegetation or some other obstruction demands that you put all your concentration into getting the fly on the water, and leaves little room for fancy casts.

The arc is almost exclusively an evening ploy, when the light is going and the sedge is up; and it demands a buoyant, well-oiled fly that will float on its hackle-points. It is a simple business. Cast down-and-across, to a position slightly upstream of your fish, and a little to the far side of him (Fig. 53). Hold the rod in such a way as to allow the fly to be drawn around in an arc, a foot upstream of the fish's nose. Expect a take at any point on the arc – and expect it to be savage, when it comes.

Just occasionally, no contact will be made on the rise. But far more often, if you give him a foot of slack before tightening, the fish will be on. Again, it is common for a fish risen in this way to hook itself. The take to the fly drifted around as described is the nearest thing to a smash-take that the river angler can expect to receive.

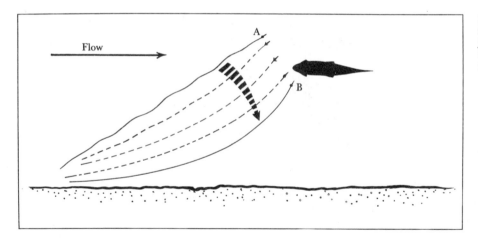

Flow

A

B

Fig. 53 The downstream arc: Cast to A above the fish and on his distant side. Allow the fly to swing just upstream of his position, B, and drop the rod the moment he takes. Then tighten carefully but firmly.

Nothing that we have said here about the downstream dry fly is intended to encourage prospecting for fish, even on those waters where downstream fishing is allowed (much less, heaven forbid, on waters where any form of downstream fishing is banned).

The downstream dry fly as we have discussed it is intended as a specific, sporting, skilful medicine, for individually located trout – just as every other tactic that we have discussed in these pages is intended for individually located fish. In the hands of a sporting and skilful angler, the downstream dry fly is a rewarding supplement to its traditional forebear.

Credit for bringing the technique to the fore in modern literature must unstintingly go to the brilliant American writer, Leonard M. Wright, Jnr. Indeed, it was after a meeting with Wright in the United States, that BC instigated our own experiments. Wright enlarges upon the technique in his splendid book *Fishing the Dry Fly as a Living Insect*, a work we can unreservedly recommend, even to the most dedicated of traditional anglers.

Wright is a sizzling writer; one of those rare men who dips his pen not into ink, but into electrical sparks. Why, he once wrote an article entitled "Isaac Who?"

Midge fishing

There are many species of very tiny flies of both an aquatic and terrestrial nature which find their way into or onto the water. Of these, the two main Families of interest to anglers are the Chironomids and the Reed Smuts. The Reed Smuts (*Simulium* spp:) have been known to flyfishers for centuries. In ancient angling literature they were often referred to as the "Black Curse" because when trout were found rising to them, the fish were impossible to catch: in those days hooks small enough to dress suitable artificials upon were unobtainable. Even today the smallest hooks available are still too large to match these extremely tiny naturals. However, provided the difficult technique of dressing a suitable pattern on a size 26 or 28 hook can be mastered, it is possible to take the occasional smutting trout on very fine tackle.

The Americans have developed this style of fishing – which they refer to as "midge fishing" – to a fine art, utilizing wands of split cane varying between $6\frac{1}{2}$ ft and $7\frac{1}{2}$ ft, weighing between one and three ounces. The reel and line are scaled down to match the rod, and the leader has a point or tippet testing between $\frac{3}{4}$ lb and 2 lb.

Many anglers in America consider midge fishing to be the cream of the sport. They consider that it tests the skill of the angler to the ultimate degree, because on such fine tackle there can be no question of dictating the fight to the trout: all that can be done is (hopefully!) to make contact without breaking, to keep in contact, hopefully to steer the fish clear of snags, and gradually to tire him out.

The Americans use these same tactics to trout rising to Chironomid (midge) pupae, as these tiny creatures drifting down in the surface film are common on many of their alkaline streams. Even in the United Kingdom the Chironomids are much more common and widespread than they used to be, and we have had some exciting times fishing to trout that have been feeding upon them.

The larvae of the Chironomids live in the mud or silt on the river bed, and their sharp increase during the last decade or so, particularly on our limestone and chalk streams, is no doubt due to twin causes: to an increase in organic pollution, and to silt deposits resulting from a decreased flow as a consequence of water abstraction.

Our most common pupae seem to be about 3 mm in length, and they vary in colour according to species from green to orange-brown to almost black. They may be imitated satisfactorily with pupa patterns dressed to match the colours of the naturals on sizes 18 or 20 hooks; and they can be suggested in emergency by equally small nymph patterns. These relatively small pupae drift down with the current just below the surface film, and for this reason they are virtually impossible to see. Unfortunately, the emergence of the adult is equally difficult to spot, as it ascends rapidly after ecdysis. If a trout is seen lying high in the water and to be sipping down apparently invisible flies, it is almost certain to be feeding on either smuts or midge pupae.

We would add one word of caution. In our view, the persistent use of tiny rods and gossamer leaders to large fish regardless of the circumstances, is not simply an affectation, but an *unsporting* affectation. No fish should be cast to with tackle clearly unlikely to land it, in the circumstances in which the fish is found.

Lovetalk . . . a moment of intimacy by the side of a trout stream

PART FOUR

Imitation

Man, trout and fly

12 The search for truth

Introduction: Towards the perfect fly

The perfect fly has not yet been invented, and we doubt that it ever will be. Perhaps this is just as well, as one of the most fascinating aspects of fly-fishing is the constant challenge and fun derived from experimenting at the fly-tying vice. There is no doubt, however, that the recent spread of fly-fishing throughout the world, combined with the proliferation of synthetic materials that have appeared on the market during the last two decades, has seen tremendous advances in fly design. Indeed, it is probably true to say that so far as the sub-surface fly is concerned, we are now far closer to the perfect fly than ever before. So lifelike are many modern nymph and pupa patterns that, if one were to remove the points and bends of the hooks, it would be difficult to tell the naturals and the artificials apart.

However, perfect physical representation is by no means the complete answer to the angler's problem, as many of our leading fly dressers have realized. It has been proved beyond reasonable doubt that patterns which emphasize or *exaggerate* key features of the natural, are often more effective than patterns which simply *look* like the natural. In addition to this, we all know that at times it is often possible to fish successfully, imitative patterns in a completely uncharacteristic way – in particular, to fish them very much faster than the naturals could move. So the problem is complex, and many factors must be taken into account by a fly-dresser who is striving for perfection.

As a result of the considerable research undertaken in the writing of this volume, we have come to the conclusion that by far the most difficult problem facing the fly-dresser is the development of successful patterns to represent the many species of *winged* naturals taken by the trout on the surface. The development of patterns to be fished underwater is simply (!) a matter of direct physical likeness, combined with correct animation in the right place, at the right time, at the correct depth.

The problem of presenting a hook adorned with feather, fur and tinsel *on the surface* in a manner calculated to deceive a wary trout, has been a challenge for the fly-fisher since the evolution of our sport.

The fly-fishing historians have established that the floating fly began to be developed seriously during the first half of the nineteenth century, partly as a result of more sophisticated hooks. (Prior to this time the hooks in general use were too crude and heavy to float, even when dressed with the most buoyant of materials.) From these early beginnings progress was gradually made; but it was not until the great yet controversial figure of F.M. Halford burst upon the angling scene in the latter part of the century that the floating fly as we know it today, first appeared. His first book, *Floating Flies and How to Dress Them*, was perhaps the greatest milestone of angling history, and the cult of dry fly purism that stemmed from his work is with us in many areas today. The many delicate and lifelike patterns he developed were masterpieces of the fly-tyer's art, and some of his dressings are still widely used.

Extraordinary though Halford's patterns were, the great man unfortunately made the mistake of matching the colours of his artificials to those of the naturals viewed from above, in direct light against a white background. In addition to this, many of the body materials that he chose – floss silk, horsehair, quill and the like – were opaque; and viewed from below the surface against direct light, these are dull and "lifeless". It was not until the early 1920s, when J.W. Dunne launched his book *Sunshine and the Dry Fly*, that the first real departures began to appear.

At the time Dunne's book caused a sensation, for apart from rejecting the Halford type of opaque body, he advanced a new theory in favour of completely translucent bodies. Not only did he write a quite brilliant thesis supporting his ideas, but he also provided a whole new range of patterns. When viewed from below directly against strong sunlight, the bodies of Dunne's flies were translucent – a feat he achieved by painting his hooks white, winding on bodies of special cellulite silks and then anointing them with paraffin. Unfortunately for Dunne, his patterns did not survive. While in practice they caught trout, results over several years indicated that they were little more effective than standard patterns, and much more time-consuming to dress. They died a natural death.

More recently we have seen the advent of fluorescent materials, and in the 1960s two specialized books were published on this fascinating subject, explaining both the theory and the use of them in the bodies of artificials. The first book, written by Joseph Keen, was called *Fluorescent Flies*. It was closely followed by a work by Thomas Clegg entitled *The Truth about Fluorescents*. The basis of both books centres upon the use of judicious amounts of fluorescents mixed in with standard body materials. While we have no sort of ethical objection to this, in practice the difficulty lies in deciding upon the colours to be used. *Our* experiments with the bodies of natural flies floating on the surface and viewed from underwater as the trout would see them, indicate that fly bodies appear at times translucent and at other times opaque, depending upon their position in the window, and the amount and angle of the light. As a direct result of this we have come to the conclusion that dubbed bodies of fur or herl – the traditional materials – are probably the best materials available at the moment, for meeting these varying conditions. As the ancients said, they give the body a lifelike sparkle, are reasonably translucent, and they are very receptive to flotant. We also believe that there is a place for quill. Although opaque, quill bodies are acceptable for spinner patterns as they are usually encountered by the trout either early or late in the day, under poorer conditions of light.

Having considered some of the problems facing the fly-dresser in respect of the bodies of floating flies, let us now look at the most difficult problem of all – that of dressing the artificial so that it will sit high upon the surface with the body barely touching it: in the way, in other words, that the natural fly appears to the trout in its lie.

The natural fly, particularly the upwinged dun when it emerges on the surface, floats high and dry like thistledown; and unless the surface film is very thin, it is able to support its weight on its legs, and to keep most or all of its body clear. As described in the chapter on the vision of the trout and made clear by our photographs, the dun is all but invisible to the trout while in the mirror, apart from the tiny dimples of light made by its feet where they touch the water. It will be realized that to produce the same effect with a conventionally dressed artificial is all but impossible, because the physical weight of the hook drags the body down into the surface. What is more, the traditional hackle wound around the shank behind the eye to represent the legs and wings of the natural, pierces the film in an unnatural way, and also dominates the body colour.

Over the years the attempts that have been made to overcome some of the problems involved in all of this, are legion. In the early part of this century a Dr Baigent developed a new series of patterns called "refracta flies", the design of which called for a fine sharp cock hackle, very short in the flue, to represent the legs. Over this he wound a hackle very long and fine in the flue to give floatability. While this met some of the shortcomings, it still did not prevent the hook bend dragging the tail of the fly down into the water; and his flies also eventually fell out of favour. The palmer pattern represents another stab at the problem. These patterns, with the hackle wound spirally for the full length of the body, have always been popular. Alas, although they cock the fly nicely, they are seldom successful on smooth water as the sheer volume of hackle presents a poor silhouette. The American fly-fisher Vincent Marinaro recently developed a new style of dressing that loosely resembles the old palmered style, except that in his design the hackle is tied in and splayed unevenly towards the head and tail. Up to a point this style of dressing also is effective, particularly when dressed on the smaller-sized hooks. Again, however, it has not proved to be over-popular, perhaps because it looks untidy.

Another unconventional design that was launched many years ago was the Parachute-hackle fly, whereon the hackle was wound horizontally over the top of the body, giving the finished product a profile similar to that of a helicopter in flight. While this certainly allowed for very delicate presentation and also provided an excellent dimpled silhouette when viewed from under water, it unfortunely presented the body below the hackle, in a manner in which the natural would never be seen.

At the other extreme, artificials without any hackles at all (such as the renowned Hare's Ear) have been used for many years. Recently, two well-known American fly-fishers, Swisher and Richards, published an excellent book entitled *Selective Trout*, in which they introduced a new concept of flies without hackles. These new patterns, which they call "No-hackle Duns", are cleverly dressed with fur bodies to give floatability, and wings to give the correct silhouette. The authors state that if these are tied correctly they will float upright and are exceptionally killing. However, JG has tried them extensively, with little result. He has had great difficulty in getting this kind of fly to float upright consistently. On the other hand he *has* found them to be effective when cast to a trout that is predominantly feeding on duns trapped in the film, that have failed to hatch successfully.

Just as recently, the introduction of "keel" hooks has resulted in some interesting floating patterns, and they have certainly solved one of the major problems facing the perfectionist fly dresser – that of the bend and point of the hook hanging below the film. These hooks unfortunately, however, have one serious drawback. The low centre of gravity which causes the fly to land on the water with the hook uppermost, also means that the shank and body of the fly dressed on it, are presented through the surface film – and as we have already explained, that is a highly undesirable feature of a floating dun pattern. (It is not, of course, an undesirable feature in a fly which floats flush with the surface film and, indeed, we have capitalized upon it for some of our flush-floating new patterns.)

The slow and dextrous groping towards the perfect fly, then, has gone on even in a disciplined way, for 100 years. Against the background of such a long-marched and impressive cavalcade of inventiveness, can it be that we have something new to offer: that we have taken the art of representation of the natural fly on metal hooks, a small step further? Time alone will answer that. For the present we would be content if we have stimulated even a little new thinking on the problems involved.

13 What we set out to achieve – and why

As a consequence of our underwater experiments and observations, we have developed a series of artificial flies that are in our belief more like the real thing *as perceived by the trout*, than anything that we have seen or heard of, so far. Their design was, indeed, dictated by what we know the trout sees.*

(Let us stress, however, that in arriving at our new designs we have incorporated into our new dressing and tying techniques many of the incremental improvements that have emerged in imitative fly-dressing over the years.)

In setting out to imitate the natural *dun* with our new dressings, we were concerned to develop:

a. A fly that was a good floater;
b. A fly that would cock the right way up at least 80 per cent of the time (and that is a great deal more than can be said for many of the winged patterns that have become established in the last 100 years);
c. A fly that would give a silhouette very similar to that of the natural, when viewed from below the water;
    AND MOST IMPORTANTLY ...
d. A style of dressing that would keep the body aloft from the surface of the water;
e. *A fly that incorporated what we believe to be the two key trigger points of the rise:*
    – The star-burst of dimples created by the feet of the natural in the surface film, when seen by the fish in the mirror; and
    – Wings that would break into the ring of the trout's window, in a manner similar to the wings of the natural.

In setting out to imitate the natural spinner, we were concerned to develop a fly that met parameters (a), (b) and (c) above; and that (d) presented the body flush with the surface film, just as the natural spinner presents itself.

After a great deal of experimentation, and the rejection of many dozens of dressings, we developed a new range of patterns that met each and all of the above requirements.

These new dressings incorporate a wide range of minor subtleties.

The dun, for example (and as discussed in more detail later on) has a wing/hackle combination that controls the descent of the fly to the surface in the attitude that we want it to alight.

In the case of the spinner, there are two points that we would mention.

The first concerns the wings. The polythene wings of the spinner patterns are pock-marked with tiny holes and indentations. The reason for this is that the holes trap tiny bubbles of air and transmit light below water to the trout, exactly as do the wings of the natural spinner: wings that are criss-crossed by veins forming indentations which trap air in the same way. Without the holes, the polythene comes *close* to transmitting the correct light pattern below the surface. *With* them, the wings transmit *exactly* the same light pattern: the indentations in the polythene are our answer to the veins in the wings of the natural – and they are astonishingly effective.

The second point we would touch upon is that we have set out to improve

*We developed the range of flies discussed in these pages ourselves, as a result of our own observations and experiments. After the first impression of *The Trout & the Fly* was printed, however, it was drawn to our attention that at least two other anglers— some time before us—had arrived at a dressing of an upside-down dun which was similar (though not identical) to the one we devised. As they were faced with the same problems of optics and aerodynamics, and the range of possible solutions to these problems (once they are understood) is somewhat limited, perhaps this is not surprising. We want to give credit, therefore, at this, our first opportunity, to those anglers who preceded us. The first we understand to have been one John Slotherton, who wrote about his version of a USD fly in the Journal of the Flyfishers' Club (London) in the early months of 1933. Slotherton's dressing was picked up and repeated subsequently in books by Col Joscelyn Lane, but Slotherton was the designer. The second angler to have arrived at a similar dressing was Hal Janssen, who apparently published the results of his work (a pattern called "The Stalker") in a magazine article published in the United States some time in 1973.

the *tails* of the artificial fly. Observed from underwater, in silhouette in the window, the tails of the natural fly have a very distinctive shape: a shape that is hopelessly misrepresented by the conventional artificial tail – a group of hackle fibres bunched together.

Because the bend of the hook in our spinner floats clear of the water, and the parachute hackle/wing configuration provides adequate flotation, we have been able to give new attention to the tails: we do not require them to provide the same help to flotation, as is necessary in a standard dressing. That we have succeeded in this endeavour is, we believe, apparent from the photographs on page 92. From many positions under water our spinner pattern is virtually *indistinguishable* from the natural.

The new duns we have decided to call the Upside Down (USD for short) Paraduns. The spinner patterns, because of their wing material, we have termed the USD Poly-Spinners.

In addition to the new floating patterns designed to be fished in the upstream, dead-drift, dry-fly manner, we have also listed some high-floating patterns that are designed to be fished with movement (particularly *downstream* movement – though note our qualifications in the text, on the use of this technique).

Lastly, we have incorporated in our list several unconventional nymphs, pupae, shrimps and the like, that have proved to be very killing when fished in the manner described. Some of these patterns are original to us; others have been developed by our friends, or are established and effective older favourites.

All of the USD Paraduns and the Poly-Spinners have been developed by us in light of our observations in the laboratory and on the river; in light of the behaviour of the trout as outlined in the early and middle chapters of this book; and in light of what we now know of the vision of trout. They have been tested on a wide range of rivers – sometimes with spectacular results.

We do not claim that we have developed the perfect fly, because blissfully (we genuinely feel), there are occasions when the trout keep the final secret and our dressings do not work. On the other hand, there are many occasions on which they *do* work – and work when the conventional fly does not.

Perhaps it is here that the true value of our dressings will lie: as a selective rifle (if we may mix our metaphors) for use against those targets that the shotgun of the conventional style of dressing simply will not hit.

There can be no doubt that the conventional fly carrying a simple wound hackle, will succeed against most fish. There are other fish, however – wily, experienced, *desirable* fish – that will not fall to such a basic fly, and that want more.

Our flies have shown that they frequently can offer more: to the trout; to the angler who simply wants to catch it; and to the fly-dressing enthusiast who will obtain *his* satisfaction from tying a fly that is as close to the natural as perceived by the trout, that to the best of our knowledge is yet available.

Before embarking upon the dressings themselves, let us stress the point again: for ourselves, we do not see our new styles of dressings as supplanting the traditional fly. We see them as *supplements to* the traditional fly. And certainly we look forward to improvements being made in due course, in the kinds of materials we have used. In particular we look forward to improvements in the wing materials of the duns. It will be seen that we have used centre-sections cut from cock or hen hackles. We have chosen this material because it allowed us to apply the outward curve we needed to give the wings, if we were to control the descent of the fly to the water, and make it land right-way up. But hackle-sections have less than the total "collapsibility" that is desirable in any winging material for artificial flies, and it is here that we would like any search for alternative materials to begin.

And so to the detailed dressings.

Any moment now . . . BC concentrates on his fish
(reproduced by permission of *The Sunday Times*)

14 How to tie the new patterns

The USD Paraduns

The USD Paraduns are dressed on standard up-eye, fine-wire hooks in sizes and colours to match the hatch. The most striking aspect of them is that they are tied upside down, and stand on a parachute-hackle situated on the reverse side of the hook. We have dressed them this way as a direct consequence of our observations of the natural fly from under water (see "Vision"). The parachute style of hackling, when reversed, spreads the fibres across the surface, dimples it and gives off a sparkling refraction in a manner very similar to that created by the feet of the natural dun when seen in the mirror. *And what is more, keeps the body of the dun aloft from the surface of the water, just as the bodies of so many natural flies are kept aloft.*

The wings, which are cut from near the tips of good quality hackles with wing cutters, should be a little longer and wider than the wings in a standard dun. They are tied in on the *reverse* side to the hackle, and given a pronounced outward curve as in the wings of a Fan-Wing Mayfly. These outwardly-arched wings then act as tiny stabilizers which ensure that the pattern lands on the water with the hook point uppermost, in spite of the parachute hackle on the other side. The length of, and number of turns given to the parachute hackle are critical, as too few turns will result in an indifferent floater, while too many will cancel out the effect of the stabilizing wings. They must also be tied in evenly, and any excess hackles projecting below the horizontal plane should be trimmed or the fly will not sit *on* the surface upright. With a little experience the length and width of the wings and density of the hackle can soon be judged, and the finished fly will then land right way up better than eight times out of ten.

Some perspectives of the USD Paradun.

For the tails on the larger patterns we use two or three muskrat or mink whiskers, depending upon the number of tails that Nature has given the natural dun we are trying to represent. These should be tied in spread well apart, as in the natural fly. We feel that in our new style of pattern (which has been designed in an attempt to deceive particularly difficult trout) even this aspect of appearance is worth suggesting. (This is particularly so in the case of the spinner dressings which follow later.) Apart from this, these whisks – or the alternatives suggested – are much stronger and more durable than the traditional hackle fibres that are used for tails. While soft whiskers are in our opinion almost perfect for tails on dry flies, being strong yet very fine, supple and also tapered, on the smaller patterns of the Paraduns we have, however, found it necessary to revert to a substantial bunch of hackle fibres tied well around the bend, to ensure that the fly lands hook uppermost. On these small flies we found that the area of the wing alone was insufficient to turn the hook upside down consistently. Where whiskers are used, they can be coloured to an appropriate shade with a spirit-based, felt-tip pen.

We have listed three different dressings for this new pattern but of course, any number of patterns can be built up using the same technique, to represent the most common naturals to be found on a particular water.

Tying the USD Paraduns

It is worth stating at the outset that these flies are not the easiest of patterns to tie, and that the dresser needs all the basic skills of the trade in order to produce a good finished article. It may be most profitable in terms of time and effort, therefore, to reserve them for very special or difficult trout.

On reaching the bend of the hook with the first layer of tying silk, one should angle the shank downwards temporarily. This will greatly assist when tying in the tails which, in the case of the USD Paraduns, should be positioned well around the bend of the hook (to help it to land the right way up), and spread well apart.

This step being completed, tie in the body materials – the ribbing and whatever is being used for the actual body of the fly. Next, tie in the loop of nylon on which the Para-hackle is wound. (The best nylon that we have found for this job is "Platil Strong", as it is very much thinner than other nylons for a given breaking strain.) Once the loop is formed, tie in on the left hand side of the loop, as close as possible to it, the hackle. Make sure that it is at right angles to the hook shank, and cut off the end of the butt. At this point the body of the fly can be wound – but only up to the place where the hackle is tied in. *Do not cut off the waste: you will need it later.* Next, bring up the rib and tie in at the same place, but in this instance remove the waste.

The next operation is to turn the hook upside-down in the vice and tie in with a figure-of-eight binding the pair of cut wings, so that they are upright or sloping slightly forward and at about 45 degrees to the horizontal, giving a V-shaped silhouette. Remove the two wing-butts. Next, run a dubbing needle up the outside of each wing under a little pressure, to produce a pronounced outward curve, and then return the fly to the normal position in the vice. Now tie in the rest of the body and thorax using the body material left hanging from the earlier operation, and this time remove the waste. All that now remains is to wind the Para-hackle around the loop of nylon, to pop the end of the hackle through the loop and to pull on the nylon to close the loop and trap the hackle.

A gallows tool is of great assistance in the tying procedure.

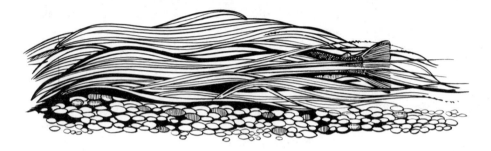

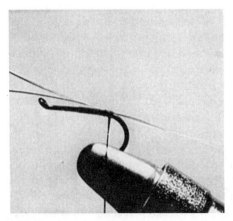

1 Take the silk along the shank and well around the bend. Secure two or three whisks or a bunch of hackle fibres, as appropriate.

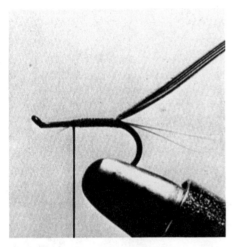

2 Secure the body material at the bend, and take the silk two-thirds of the distance back to the eye.

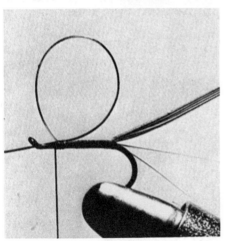

3 Tie in a loop of nylon. Do not pull it too tight.

4 Secure a good quality, short-flue hackle at right angles to the shank, as close to the bend side of the loop as possible. Trim off butt.

5 Cut the wings from near the top centre of a good quality hen hackle using a wing cutter.

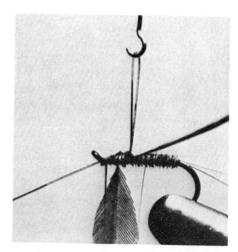

6 Reverse hook in vice (and for pattern with rib, see note 7). With figure-of-eight tying, secure a pair of cut wings in such a way that they appear as a V when viewed from eye of the hook. Cut off the two butts, and then run a dubbing needle up the outside of both wings under a little pressure, to give them a pronounced outward curve.

7 Wind the body material up to the eye, and trim off the excess. (Note: if a pattern with a rib is being dressed, this operation will have to be carried out before the wings are tied in.)

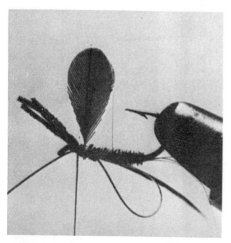

11 The completed USD Paradun.

8 Reverse the hook in the vice. Take the loop of nylon onto a gallows tool, and prepare to put two to four turns of the hackle as tightly and as low as possible around the loop.

9 Take the turns of hackle around the loop. Pass the tip through the loop, hold with the finger and thumbs (not shown here for the sake of simplicity) and begin to draw loop tight.

10 The loop is now pulled tight to trap the hackle point, and the excess hackle is trimmed. Now apply a blob of varnish where the centre of the hackle is trapped under the loop. When the varnish is dry, trim off any excess nylon from the loop, and remove any hackle fibres projecting below the horizontal.

Dressings

No.1 USD Para-Blue Winged Olive
Silk:	Orange
Hook:	12, 14 or 16 UE
Tails:	Three muskrat or mink whiskers, coloured dark olive, or bunch of hackle fibres
Body:	Natural heron herl
Wings:	Dark grey or dark blue dun
Hackle:	Rusty dun

No.2 USD Para-Olive
Silk:	Brown
Hook	12, 14 or 16 UE
Tails:	Two muskrat or mink whiskers coloured olive, or bunch of hackle fibres
Body:	Heron herl dyed olive in picric acid
Wings:	Pale blue dun
Hackle:	Olive cock

No.3 USD Para-Pale Watery
Silk:	Yellow
Hook:	16 or 17 UE
Tails:	Bunch of pale honey hackle fibres
Body:	Greyish goose primary herls
Wings:	Cream or pale blue dun
Hackle:	Rusty dun

The USD Poly-Spinners

The main features of these new spinner patterns are that they are dressed upside down as are the Paraduns, but on keel hooks; and they have wings which are formed from specially-prepared flat polythene sheet. (Before the wings are tied in they are pierced in many places to give them an uneven undersurface. This causes them to emit a similar pattern of light to that created by the veins in the wings of the natural when seen from underwater – a phenomenon described elsewhere in this volume.)

We have again used a parachute hackle, but this time it is tied in on *top* of the body along with the wings. In this position it not only closely simulates the legs of the natural fly, but allows the body – which is underneath – to sit well down in the surface film in the manner adopted by the body of the natural spinner. With this pattern we were unable to use the shape of the wings – as in the Paraduns – to ensure that the fly alighted right way up with the bend and point of the hook uppermost because, of course, the spinner wings are tied in completely flat. We therefore had to solve this problem in a different way – we used the new keel hook. This hook would have been quite inappropriate for the dun because it would have drowned the parachute hackles. It works excellently on the spinner pattern, however, because it forces the body into the surface film where we want it, and leaves the parachute hackle and flat wings on the surface to keep the fly afloat.

The polythene wings tend to spin the fly when casting, but on the small patterns this is minimal, and does not present a serious problem. On larger patterns, such as those which imitate the large Mayfly spinners, the revolving of the fly puts a sufficient twist in the leader for us to revert to the traditional hackle-point wings in these few flies. All these new spinner patterns incorporate the new-style tails as described for the Paraduns, and float similarly well with them.

Tying the USD Poly-Spinners

When it comes to tying the USD Spinners, the procedure is at first much the same as for the Duns – i.e. the tails and body materials are tied in almost up to the point where the loop on the keel side (to take the parachute hackle) is to be tied in. The fly can then be turned upside down and left that way for the remainder of the dressing.

The wings of finest gauge polythene should now be cut with a wing cutter as a joined pair (by folding the polythene over and cutting in from the edge – Fig. 54), but before tying them in they should be laid flat on a piece of heavy cardboard and pierced lightly many times with a thick but sharp needle. If done correctly the point will barely pass through the wing while the blunt angle leading to the point will produce a distinct dimple in the polythene.

The next operation is to tie in the loop of nylon around which the hackle

Fig. 54 How to cut a joined pair of polywings.

will be wound, and the body material can then be taken up to the eye and tied off. The hackle is then tied in by the butt as close to the base of the loop as possible. Two and up to five turns are now taken around the base of the loop as tightly as possible. The end or tip is now passed through the loop. The wings are also passed through the nylon loop, and the loop is then pulled tight to secure both wings and hackle. The wings should then be secured tightly with a figure-of-eight tying, care being taken not to trap any of the hackle fibres with the silk. It is important to minimize the tendency of this pattern to twist the leader by using the thinnest possible polythene, and also by cutting the wings as small as possible in keeping with the size of the pattern being dressed. (*We recommend "Denvilles Pre-waxed Nylon" for dressing all these spinner patterns.*)

1 Wind the silk down to the bend, and tie in two or three mink whiskers for the tails.

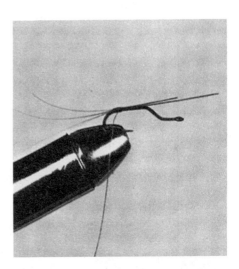

2 The tails should be spread well apart, as shown here. A blob of varnish applied to the base, will hold them in position.

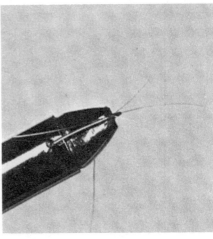

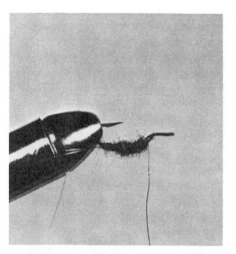

3 Reverse the hook. Dub the body material (in this case seal's fur) onto the silk, and wind along the shank to the end of the keel.

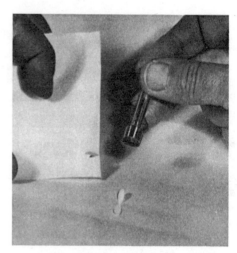

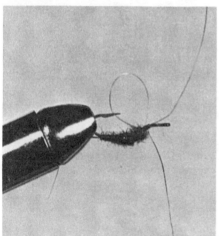

4 Tie in the loop of nylon (not too tightly) halfway up the slope from the keel to the eye. Dub a little more body material onto the silk, and take a fraction further towards the eye.

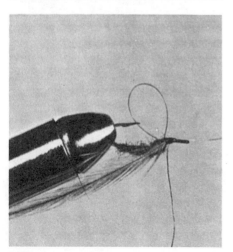

5 Tie in the hackle by the butt, as close as possible to the base of the loop. Then fit the gallows tool to the vice.

6 Cut the wings from a doubled sheet of lightest gauge polythene utilizing one of the new cutters in the appropriate size, and then pierce with a blunt needle. (The wings should be prepared beforehand.)

7 According to hook size, take between two and five turns of hackle tightly around the base of the loop, and then pass the tip through the loop. Hold the tip with finger and thumb (not shown for the sake of simplicity) until operation 8 has been completed.

8 Pass the pre-cut, thin-gauge polythene wings through the loop.

Dressings

No.1 USD Poly-Pheasant-Tail Spinner

Hook: 12 or 14 keel hooks
Silk: Orange
Tails: Two muskrat or mink whiskers coloured pale brown
Body: Pheasant-tail fibre
Wings: Polythene, cut with wing cutter
Hackle: Rusty dun cock

No.2 USD Poly-Red Spinner

Hook: 12, 14 or 16 keel hooks
Silk: Brown
Tails: Two muskrat or mink whiskers coloured pale blue
Body: Red seal's fur
Wings: As for No.1
Hackle: Pale blue dun cock

No.3 USD Poly-Yellow Boy Spinner

Hook: 14 or 16 keel hook
Silk: Yellow
Tails: Two muskrat or mink whiskers coloured pale yellow
Body: Medium yellow seal's fur
Wings: As Nos.1 & 2
Hackle : Light buff cock

No.4 USD Poly-Orange Spinner

Hook: 14 keel hook
Silk: Orange
Tails: Three muskrat or mink whiskers coloured brown
Body: Orange seal's fur
Rib: DFM orange floss
Wings: As Nos.1, 2 & 3
Hackle: Bright ginger cock

No.5 USD Sherry Spinner (Skues Type)

Hook: 14 keel hook
Silk: Orange
Tails: Three muskrat or mink whiskers coloured pale brown
Body: Orange and green seal's fur mixed with fur from a hare's poll
Rib: Fine gold wire
Wings: As for Nos.1, 2, 3 & 4
Hackle: Pale honey dun cock with dark centre

9 Pull nylon tight to secure both hackle-point and wings. Give wings extra security by binding with a figure-of-eight tying. (This is not an easy operation to perform, as the silk at each cross-over must be woven in between the hackle fibres, without trapping any of them.) Finish head with whip finish, and varnish.

The USD Mayfly Spinner

As previously mentioned, for large spinner patterns such as those to represent a spent gnat Mayfly, it is not feasible to use polythene wings. For this or similar large spinner patterns we therefore decided to revert to traditional hackle-point wings, though we still retained a keel hook to ensure as accurate a presentation as possible, from the perspective of the trout. At first glance the rather garish colours are completely out of keeping with the general run of river patterns, which tend to be rather drab. Nevertheless, the design has proved to be devastatingly effective. There can be little doubt that the hot-orange hackle gives the fly high visibility (enabling it to be picked out in a heavy fall of natural flies) while the profile of the body/wings in the mirror and the excellent silhouette in the window sustain the illusion at close quarters.

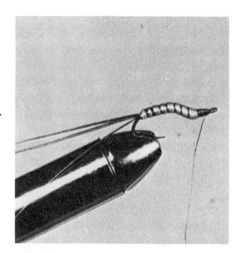

The USD Mayfly Spinner is a fairly simple pattern to dress. Take a long-shank keel hook, wind yellow tying silk along from the eye to the bend, and secure three tails of dark pheasant-tail fibres, spread well apart. Next, tie in a length of black monocord with which to rib the body, and take the silk back to the eye. The body material of white polypropylene fibres is then laid along the top of the shank, and secured with turns of silk. The silk is next taken back to the eye, the polypropylene is wound up over it, trimmed, and ribbed with the monocord. Two good-quality grizzle-hackle points are then secured with a figure-of-eight tying. The fly is completed with two turns of a hot orange hackle wound round each side of the wings and tied off at the eye. N.B. For use on rough water it is a good plan to tie in an extra hackle, preferably a grizzle.

1 Using yellow silk, tie in three dark pheasant tail fibres for the tails and a length of black mono-cord for the ribbing. Take the silk to the eye, and secure a length of white polypropylene fibres along the top of the shank to the bend. Take the silk back to the eye again.

2 Wind the polypropylene up to the eye, rib, and cut off excess materials.

3 Secure two good quality grizzle-hackle tips with a figure-of-eight tying, to lie in the spent position. Cut off the butts.

4 Select an appropriate size of hot orange cock hackle, secure in front of the wings, and then take two turns behind the wings and two in front. Tie off, clip excess, and varnish.

Dressing

Hook:	10 or 12 keel hook, long shank
Silk:	Yellow
Tails:	Three dark pheasant tail fibres
Rib:	Black monocord or silk, doubled
Body:	White polypropylene fibres
Hackle:	Hot orange and grizzle cock hackles – two turns each side of wings
Wings:	Grizzle hackle-points

The New "Suspender" Patterns

This and the following two patterns were developed in conjunction with Neil Patterson, but the original concept of utilizing a small section of nylon mesh to enclose a semi-buoyant material to assist in holding an artificial nymph in the surface film must be credited to Charles E. Brooks, the well-known American angler. Brooks refers to his pattern as the 'Natant Nylon Nymph'. While his concept is quite novel, in practice we found that the polypropylene he suggested – even when treated with a flotant – still did not give as much buoyancy as we wanted. After much experimentation we decided that a modern, closed-cell foam commonly referred to as *Ethafoam* was by far the most buoyant material available. A small square of this cut from a sheet and then trimmed with hackle scissors into a ball provided the perfect answer. With a ball of this material enclosed in the nylon mesh (ladies' nylon stockings provide the ideal material; and how you get them is your own affair), and with that ball mounted in the appropriate position on top of the hook, we now had a pattern that would float all day if necessary, even in the roughest of water. Furthermore, we also had a material that could be coloured successfully and quickly with a spirit-based felt-tip pen. As Brooks suggests, this little ball tied on top of the shank is not at all out of place, because it closely stimulates the thorax and wings pads found on all hatching nymphs (and also, as we were later to realize, when tied in over the eye of the hook, the white coloration of the *Ethafoam* through the mesh also tellingly suggests the large tuft of white breathing filaments found on most mature midge pupae). The name decided upon for this new series of patterns is, we hope, self-explanatory in more senses than one.

Suspender Nymph

The dressing we give here is for a pattern to represent the many species of olive nymphs that are common on many rivers. By the simple expedient of varying the body colour, other species may be represented. The size of the ball of *Ethafoam* mounted on top of the shank can vary in diameter from ⅛th inch up to ¼ inch depending upon the size of the hook used, or the degree of buoyancy required. As a general rule, however, unless for a specific reason the artificial is required to ride high in the surface film, we suggest that the ball is kept as small as possible consistent with providing sufficient buoyancy to float the hook being used.

The dressing procedure is as follows. Wind brown tying silk in the usual manner down the shank to the bend, where three or four green-dyed golden pheasant tippets are tied in spread well apart to represent the small barred tails of the natural nymph. Next cut a square of *Ethafoam* to the appropriate size and trim into a small ball. We now come to perhaps the most interesting part, which is to beg, borrow, steal or win a lady's nylon stocking (it's more fun if you do not rush this stage). From this, cut a section of mesh between three-quarters and one inch square. In the centre of this place your small ball of *Ethafoam* and then pull the mesh around it until it is totally enclosed, as in a pouch. This is then tied on top of the body a third of the way along the shank from the eye, by binding down the loose ends of mesh, making sure that you take the silk as tightly up to the ball as possible. The excess mesh may then be trimmed. Secure a length of silver wire for ribbing the body, and then dub the silk with the olive seal's fur or *Sealex* from which the body is formed, and wind up to the eye and tie off. The body should then be ribbed. The final operation is to tie in a grizzle hackle sloping well back behind the eye under the wing pad or ball, and then to colour the ball dark brown with a felt-tip pen.

Dressing

Hook:	14 or 16 DE
Silk:	Brown
Tails:	Three olive dyed golden pheasant tippets
Rib:	Silver wire
Body:	Olive seal's fur or *Sealex*
Hackle:	Grizzle
Wing pad:	*Ethafoam* ball enclosed in nylon mesh and coloured dark brown – we suggest Pantone shade 499M

Mayfly Suspender Nymph

Dressed as a semi-floating pattern, it is based on the same principle as the preceding artificial: in other words, a ball of *Ethafoam* supports the head above the surface, yet allows the tails and body to hang at an angle below the surface in a perfectly natural manner. In addition, as this is a much larger pattern and therefore more obvious to the trout, we have endeavoured to provide as lifelike a pattern as possible insofar as appearance and colour are concerned. First of all, the three medium-length tails formed from the tips of cream-coloured ostrich herl should be tied in spread well apart (a small blob of varnish at the joints of these tails will *keep* them separated). The small ball of *Ethafoam* cut to size and enclosed in nylon stocking mesh is now tied in as described in the hatching nymph pattern, a short distance back from the eye.

Next, tie in brown monocord or heavy silk for subsequent use as the body ribbing. A mixture of white, tan and yellow seal's fur is then dubbed onto the tying silk and wound up the shank to the eye, and tied in but not trimmed off. Bring up the rib and tie in. The remainder of the body material is now wound in to form a thorax on each side of the ball, and is picked out to simulate legs.

1 Wind the brown tying silk down to the bend and secure the tips of three cream-coloured ostrich herls to form the tails. Apply a dab of varnish to hold the tails well apart.

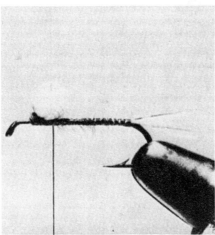

2 Wind the silk two-thirds of the way back along the shank, and secure a ball of Ethafoam in its pouch of nylon mesh, on top of the hook, at the point shown. Trim the excess mesh.

3 Take the silk back to the bend and secure a length of brown monocord. Dub the silk with tan and yellow seal's fur.

Dressing

Hook:	12DE long shank
Silk:	Brown
Tails:	Three tips of cream ostrich herl
Rib:	Brown monocord or silk
Body:	Seal's fur mixed $\frac{1}{2}$ white, $\frac{1}{4}$ tan, $\frac{1}{4}$ yellow
Wing cases:	*Ethafoam* ball enclosed in nylon mesh and coloured brown (Pantone 464M)
Thorax:	As body

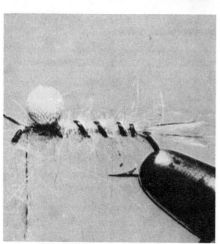

4 Wind the seal's fur back to the eye to form the body, but do not trim off. Rib the body with the monocord, and cut off excess.

5 Wind the seal's fur back and forth either side of the ball to build up a thorax, and secure at the eye with a whip finish. Varnish. Pick out the thorax with a dubbing needle, and colour the ball with a felt-tipped pen.

Suspender Hatching Midge Pupa

This is a pattern specifically dressed to imitate medium-to-small-sized chironomids hatching in the surface film. It is very effective when fished on light tackle to trout observed sipping down these small pupae – an increasingly common sight on many rivers. First, fine 'midge' tying silk is taken down the shank and well round the bend of the hook, where the rib of silver wire is secured. The body material of green acetate floss is then wound to the top of the bend, where a small strip of plastic is tied in to project backwards for about a quarter of an inch. The floss is then continued two thirds along the shank where it is secured and the excess is cut off. The body is then ribbed. A tiny ball of *Ethafoam* enclosed in nylon mesh is then tied in immediately behind the eye but projecting forward over it. The thorax, formed from one dark-brown condor herl or dyed turkey herl is now tied in immediately behind the ball to complete the fly.

Dressing

Hook:	16 or 18 DE
Silk:	Fine midge
Body:	Green acetate floss
Rib:	Silver wire
Shuck case:	Small section of plastic mayfly body
Thorax:	One dark brown condor herl or dyed turkey
Wing case:	Small ball of *Ethafoam* enclosed in nylon mesh

The Caenis Spinner

This is a new pattern developed by our very good friend, the gifted fly-dresser Stewart Canham. JG looks upon this as his standard pattern when these tiny spinners are on the water. It has proved a killing dressing even when no naturals are on the water. It is a straightforward fly to dress, in spite of its exceptionally small size. With white tying silk secure the three tails, which should be tied in spread well apart. Follow with the body material, which is a narrow strip cut from a white polythene bag. Wind this two thirds up the shank and tie in. Follow with one brown condor or turkey herl to form the thorax. The wings, which are cut with the smallest size of wing cutter from a white hen hackle, are then tied on in the spent fashion. Finally, tie in a white cock hackle which should be short in the flue, and trim off the bottom edge.

Dressing

Hook:	18 UE standard
Silk:	Fine midge
Tails:	Three fibres from a white cock hackle
Body:	White polythene
Thorax:	One brown condor or turkey herl
Wings:	White hen hackles, cut with wing cutter
Hackle:	White cock hackle, trimmed on bottom edge

Hatching Sedge Pupa

It has probably been noticed that many of our new dressings are tied on slightly smaller hooks than would normally be expected. This is because our underwater experiments show that the majority of artificials are dressed far too large accurately to suggest the naturals they are meant to represent. This pattern continues the theme, and on this size of hook is much more in keeping with the size of the average pupa. We have endeavoured to follow the silhouette of the natural as closely as possible, and while the two dressings we suggest are tied in colours to match the most common naturals, they may be dressed in other shades or on different-sized hooks if so desired. We dress these pupae in both weighted and unweighted versions, and although they may be used on still water they have been specifically developed for river fishing. We use the unweighted pattern at dusk fished just below the surface, when emergence of the natural is often at its peak. It is often more effective when fished with a well-timed twitch to provide animation, but this is, of course, only applicable where the rules of the water allow movement of the fly. The weighted pattern we use during the day, fished as one would normally use pupae of the day-hatching species. It is a rather difficult pattern to dress, as it is important to tie in the materials in the correct proportions. First, tie in a length of silver wire at the bend for the rib, followed by the body of medium olive or orange seal's fur. The body material should be wound slightly over half-way along the shank and temporarily tied off. The rib should then be wound over the body, tied in and trimmed off. The seal's fur is then continued a little more thickly to the eye to form the thorax. Behind the eye, the wings of grey mallard are secured alongside the thorax, with the tips projecting backwards below the body. Two antennae of brown mallard fibres are then tied in on top, to slope well back over the body. The final operation is to tie in the legs of green-dyed partridge sloping back under the body. When dressing this pattern it is important to leave sufficient room between the eye and the thorax material to secure neatly the legs, antennae and wings.

Dressing

Hook:	12 DE standard
Body:	Medium olive seal's fur
Rib:	Silver wire
Wings:	Grey mallard wing quill sections
Antennae:	Two brown mallard fibres
Thorax:	As body
Legs:	Green dyed grey partridge hackle, tied in "false"
Silk:	Orange

Orange version: as above, but with orange seal's fur and brown partridge hackle.

The Mating Shrimp

On some rivers trout will feed avidly on freshwater shrimps during July and August, a time of the year when these crustaceans have donned their mating dress and taken on a distinct pinky-orange hue. Our patterns to imitate the shrimp are dressed in several sizes and weights, partly because the naturals vary in size, and partly to enable us to fish various depths of water. Shrimps mostly live on the bed of the river among gravel, stones, weeds or detritus, and when one finds a trout feeding upon them there, it is necessary to get the artificial right down to the fish at its depth in the water. A trout feeding upon shrimps can be quickly recognized as it nearly always lies fairly close to the bottom at a slight angle, with its head down and its tail slightly up. The materials we have used for the body match, when wet, the different mating colours of many shrimps very well, and these designs, used in the right conditions, are probably the most killing patterns we carry. We have developed two basic patterns – one used by JG, and one by BC. We will begin with JG's because that is the most complex. BC's simpler version, which follows a broadly similar tying procedure, except for the manner of weighting, is noted at the bottom. Wind the orange tying silk down the shank to the bend, and then secure a strip of thin lead (about 4 in long and two or three times as wide as the shank of the hook being used) along the top of the shank from the bend almost to the eye. This is then folded and refolded backward and forward, rapidly reducing the length of each fold to build up to both the necessary weight and the typical hump-backed shape of the shrimp. Each fold is secured with the silk in turn. When the desired shape and weight (determined by the number of laps) is achieved, trim off the excess lead and whip from eye to bend with the silk. Next, take the silk well round the bend, and tie in a strip of PVC or strong polythene. This should be cut slightly longer than the shank, about $\frac{1}{4}$ in wide in the centre and tapering slightly at each end. A mixture of seal's fur or *Sealex* is then dubbed onto the silk and wound up to the eye and tied in. Finally, the PVC or polythene is stretched over the top, secured at the eye, and trimmed. Pick out the seal's fur below the body only, with a dubbing needle. (Note that the above style of leading is used to simulate the typical hump-backed shape of the shrimp as it crawls on the river bed. To imitate the shrimp stretched out swimming just off the bottom, the lead strip tied in along the top of the shank is still lapped back and forth but in this case each lap is only very slightly reduced in length. BC, who is all for an easy life, saves time with his pattern by simply winding lead wire along the shank.)

1 Take the tying silk along the shank to the bend, and secure a long, narrow strip of lead foil. Lay the foil along the top of the shank, secure with wide turns of silk, and then fold the lead back over itself, and repeat turns of silk.

2 Fold the lead back and forth in ever-shorter lengths, fastening each with wide turns of silk. When the shape shown in the photograph has been achieved, trim off the excess lead, and whip the whole body closely with silk. End with the silk part-way round the bend.

3 Secure a wide strip of PVC well round the bend. Secure a length of the appropriate ribbing wire at the same point.

Dressing

Hook: 8, 10 or 12 standard, wide gape
Silk: Orange, green, olive, or yellow (use colour to "code" a particular weight of lead)
Back: Clear polythene or PVC
Rib: Oval silver wire (JG version), fine gold wire (BC version)
Body: (JG version) Seal's fur mixed: – 60% olive, 30% brown, 10% DFM pink; or (BC version) – 80% olive plus 20% amber

4 Dub the silk with the appropriate seal's fur mixture, wind it over the lead to behind the eye, and rib with wire. Cut off waste wire.

5 Stretch the PVC over the top of the body, secure at the eye, trim off waste, and build up a neat head. Varnish.

Note: The above dressing, and the photographs, are for JG's shrimp. The same procedure is followed for BC's shrimp (see detailed dressing), after the simpler leading stage for BC's shrimp has been completed.

The Goddard Caddis (G & H Sedge)

This is not a new pattern, but one that JG developed several years ago for still water fishing. It is now an established favourite with lake fishermen, and has proved to be equally profitable for river anglers as well. The main feature of this pattern is the body of deer hair, which is trimmed to shape after it is tied in to represent the wings of the natural. This technique provides an excellent silhouette, when viewed from underwater, and the deer hair is extremely buoyant. If it is well soaked in flotant before use, the fly will float for several hours even in the roughest water. For still water JG dresses it on a longshank hook, size No.8 or 10, but for rivers we have found it is most effective on smaller hooks used as a traditional dry fly, cast up or across to rising fish. It may be dressed in colours other than those given here, to represent different species.

Tying the G & H Sedge

Unfortunately this is a difficult and time-consuming pattern to dress, even for the proficient fly-dresser. After winding the green tying silk round the hook shank at the bend, tie in a doubled length of the same silk, to be used later for the underbody. The main body material of deer's hair is then spun on, using a similar technique as for the Muddler Minnow, starting at the bend and working down towards the eye. Several spinnings of this hair are necessary, each new one being pressed close up to the last until the hook is completely palmered with deer hair. The hair should then be clipped with sharp scissors removing all the hair underneath and part-way along each side, and tapering towards the eye to give the correct sedge silhouette when viewed from below. Two rusty dun cock hackles are then tied in together at the eye, leaving (optional) the stripped butts protruding over the eye to simulate the two antennae of the natural sedge fly. The top of this hackle is then trimmed. Finally, dark green seal's fur (or any other colour needed to match the hatch) is twisted in between the double length of green silk which was originally tied in and left hanging at the bend. This is then pulled taut under the trimmed deer hair body and whipped in at eye.

Dressing

Hook:	UE long shank, size 10 and 12
Silk:	Green
Body:	Several bunches of deer hair – spun on and trimmed to shape, as described above
Underbody:	Dark green seal's fur (but see above)
Hackle:	Two rusty dun cock, trimmed off on top

The Gerroff

This is a new pattern that JG originally devised for river fishing, to combat the peculiar conditions which applied during the height of the 1976 season, when Britain was affected by the worst drought for more than two centuries. At this time the flow on most rivers was reduced almost to a standstill. Normal weighted nymph patterns were not very effective, because on water lacking reasonable movement, they sank too quickly. On the other hand, unweighted patterns were even less effective, for as a result of the general lack of surface fly, all the trout were feeding on or close to the bottom. We therefore came to the conclusion that a special pattern was required: one that would sink (but very, very slowly) and at the same time would look like an item of food to the trout. A shrimp-type dressing was decided upon as being generally attractive to most fish; and we sought to achieve the desired rate of sinking, by marrying a buoyant body material to a style of tying that used only half the length of hook shank. This did solve the problem, and in addition had the added attraction of providing us with a pattern that presented a small silhouette, yet a relatively big hook on which to hold a large trout. Whether or not it was the size or appearance of the pattern or the materials chosen to dress it we do not know, but it certainly proved to be a most successful pattern. On its very first outing it accounted for two limit bags of 12 trout for two rods totalling 49 lb, and since then has accounted for many other heavy bags from both rivers and still waters. As far as still water is concerned we would not recommend it for large reservoirs or deep waters, but for small relatively clear waters it is exceptionally killing. Mounted alone on the point with a floating line it should be cast out either in the vicinity of a trout which can be seen feeding underwater, or alongside weed beds where trout are likely to be feeding. The "plop!" entry as it hits the surface will often attract fish from several yards, and as it slowly sinks one can often watch the trout swim up and suck it in. So confidently do trout accept this fly that many times we have watched small unwanted trout swim up and take it into their mouths, chew on it, spit it out and then take it again and again – all before it could reach the larger fish it had been cast to. In fact it was because of this that it received its rather peculiar name. The water we were fishing was stocked with more than its fair share of small trout, and the challenge was to pick out the larger fish from among them. BC spent most of one morning pulling the fly out of the mouths of the eager, smaller fish and shouting "Get off". By lunch time this had become abbreviated to "Gerroff". The exclamation was adopted as a name, which has since stuck.

The Gerroff is an exceptionally easy pattern to tie. With brown silk tie in a strip of PVC or polythene half way down the hook shank. Next, mix olive-brown seal's fur with some fluorescent pink (three parts brown to one pink) and dub onto the silk. This should then be wound on to the shank up to the eye, with a slight taper at each end. To complete the fly, stretch the PVC over the top of the body material and tie in at the eye.

Dressing

Hook:	DE size 10 to 14 with slightly longer shank than a standard hook
Silk:	Brown
Body:	Olive brown and fluorescent pink seal's fur, mixed three parts brown to one pink
Wing case:	Strip of PVC (the new latex material may be used in place of PVC)

N.B. *This pattern is only effective in still or very slow moving water.*

The PVC Nymph

This is one of our oldest patterns, one that JG originally developed as a copy of many of the olive nymphs found in rivers; but in recent years it has proved to be equally effective on still water when used to represent the nymphs of the pond and lake olives. At the time it was first evolved, Sawyer's Pheasant Tail Nymph was rapidly increasing in popularity, and while this proved to be an excellent artificial to represent many of the darker species of nymphs, particularly when fished with the induced take method, JG felt it was the wrong colour for a dead-drift presentation when olive nymphs were hatching. The new pattern, which was based on Sawyer's use of copper wire, immediately proved to be a resounding success, and since those early days has steadily increased in popularity. It has accounted for many large trout on both rivers and still waters. The PT Nymph and the PVC Nymph can be carried together, as they are complementary.

The PVC Nymph is not a particularly easy pattern to dress, as it takes a little practice to get the proportions of the materials right. Take a length of copper wire and build up a substantial thorax, as in a PT Nymph, a little way behind the eye, and then continue with a single winding down to the bend, and cut off the surplus. Brown tying silk should then be wound on at the bend, where a strip of PVC $\frac{1}{8}$th inch wide is secured, followed by three strands of olive-dyed condor herl. Three golden pheasant tippets dyed olive green are then tied in, with the fine tips protruding about $\frac{3}{16}$ths of an inch at the rear, to form the barred tails. The silk is then wound up to the eye, and is followed by the three strands of olive-dyed condor which are wound evenly over the copper wire up to eye, for securing. Next, the silk is taken back behind the thorax and the PVC strip is then wound over the condor, up to the thorax, and tied in. Finally, the silk is taken back to the eye where the wing cases of two or three dark pheasant tail fibres are doubled and redoubled over the top of the thorax, and secured.

Notes

1. A strip of latex may be used in place of the PVC, but we prefer PVC because it has less stretch, and so is easier to cut and to handle. More importantly it is less opaque, so the body colour shows through better.
2. For tiny unweighted patterns dressed on size 18 hooks or smaller, we dispense with the copper wire and form a simple thorax from dark-brown dyed turkey herl strands. Very tiny dressings can be most effective for trout feeding just below the surface.

Dressing

Hook:	DE size 12 to 17
Silk:	Brown
Tails:	Formed from the tips of three golden pheasant tippets dyed olive green
Underbody and thorax:	Copper wire
Overbody and thorax:	Three strands of olive or olive brown condor herl or substitute
Body covering:	A $\frac{1}{8}$th inch wide strip of PVC wound and over-lapped up to thorax
Wing pads:	Two or three strands of dark pheasant-tail herl

The Grey Fox Variant

This is an American pattern, but used at the right time it is so effective that we felt we just had to include it. The pattern was originally developed by Preston Jennings, but in more recent years it has been improved by that master fisherman and fly-dresser Art Flick. Flick has stated in print that he would not hesitate to name this pattern as his choice, if he were restricted to one artificial for the entire season. The Grey Fox Variant really is a marvellous pattern, especially during the latter half of the season when the natural sedge flies are most prevalent. It is often effective fished as a traditional dry fly on the dead drift. However, it is most killing when animated and drawn lightly over the surface in the vicinity of a rising trout. Due to the method of tying in the hackles, it sits up high on the points the moment it is moved, and imitates marvellously the newly-hatched sedge fly fluttering on the surface in an effort to become airborne. This dressing is particularly effecive at dusk. Cast across the river in the faster stretches, and dropped at the heads of runs, pockets or eddies between weed beds or rocks, it is astonishing how many trout it will rise. The Grey Fox Variant may be tied on several sizes of hooks to match whatever species of sedge may be hatching at the time. It is a tricky pattern to dress. The procedure is as follows. Commence by tying in a tail of six or eight honey dun cock fibres, which should be longer than normal to balance the large hackles to be used at the eye. Next, tie in a light ginger quill that has been stripped and well soaked to form the body. This is only wound about a third of the way up the hook shank from the bend, before being tied in and trimmed. Next, the hackles. The hackles for this pattern must be good quality cock, sharp without too much flue. They should be at least three sizes larger than those used on a normal pattern, and all should have the same size or length of flue. Tie in three hackles beside the body on top of the shank, with the butts pointing towards the eye, and the bright side of the hackle facing away. The nearest hackle should be dark ginger, the middle grizzle and the far one light ginger. Trim the butts. Spin the dark ginger hackle with the bright side towards the eye, making the turns as close together as possible. Tie off, trim excess hackle, and then do the same with the grizzle hackle, winding it over the top of the dark ginger hackle. Tie in and wind the light ginger hackle in the same way in tight turns over the top of the other two. Finally, trim off any hackles out of place and varnish body and head well.

Dressing

Hook:	U/E sizes 10, 12 and 14
Silk:	Yellow
Tail:	6 or 8 fibres of honey dun cock
Body:	Light ginger quill
Hackles:	Good quality cock – dark ginger, light ginger and grizzle

The Sunk Spinner

As explained elsewhere, some female spinners crawl deep down into the water to lay their eggs and in areas where this happens trout often lie in wait and feed on the spent flies drifting down with the current once their task has been completed. The Sunk Spinner, a dressing originated by Neil Patterson, has proved very successful in imitating the flies at this stage. It should be cast well upstream of a feeding fish to allow it plenty of time to sink to his level. If it is not taken dead-drift, a slight lift of the rod-top will impart just enough movement to attract special attention to it.

Tying the Sunk Spinner

Tie in two hare's whiskers and a length of monofilament well round the bend of the hook. Clip off one of the hare's whisker-butts, leaving the other at the bend of the hook to act as ribbing. Leaving the silk at the bend, tie in the copper wire independently, building up a thorax at the head and bringing it down once over the body and back. Clip off. Wind the silk to behind the thorax. Rib the body with the hare's whisker butt, and tie in at the thorax. Cover with tight turns of monofilament, and tie in at the thorax. Tie in three cock pheasant-tail fibres behind the thorax. Tie in badger hackle in front of the thorax, wind two turns over the thorax and tie in behind it. Clip off hackle point. Bring the pheasant-tail fibres over the thorax and hackle twice, tying in each time with silk. Cut off any hackle fibres underneath the hook so that the fibres which remain form spent wings. Varnish the head.

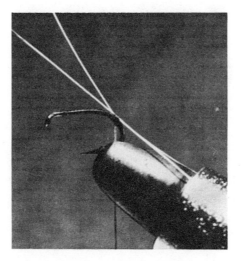

1 Take the crimson tying silk down the shank and well round the bend of the hook. Tie in two hare's whiskers for the tails, trim the butt of one of them, and leave the butt of the other for use as ribbing.

2 Tie in a length of 6 lb monofilament. Leave the silk at the bend, and wind on a length of copper wire independently along the shank to the eye.

3 Use the wire to form a substantial thorax behind the eye, and remove excess. Bring the silk over the wire body from the bend to immediately behind the thorax.

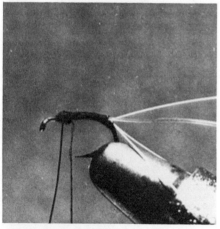

4 Rib the body with the hare's whisker, secure behind the thorax, and trim off excess. Bring the monofilament up in tight turns over the body, tie in behind the thorax, and trim off waste.

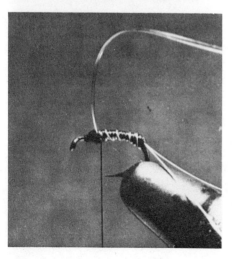

5 Tie in three or four dark pheasant tail fibres behind the thorax. Tie a badger hackle in front of the thorax, and trim off butt.

6 Wind two or three turns of the hackle around the thorax, secure with silk behind the eye, and trim hackle tip.

7 Double and redouble the pheasant tail fibres over the thorax and hackle, secure at the eye and trim off waste. Form a tapered head with the silk, and varnish. Trim off any hackle fibres above the horizontal.

8 Reverse the hook in the vice, and trim off all hackle fibres on the underside of the hook, so that those fibres remaining form spent wings.

9 Apply a dab of varnish to the base of the tails, to keep them well apart.

Dressing

Hook:	12–14 Mustad, short-shank (or 14–16 of any other)
Tying silk:	Crimson
Tails:	Two hare's whiskers (if unobtainable, use two lengths of white horsehair)
Rib:	Butt of one of the hare's whiskers (or horsehair)
Underbody:	Dark red enamel copper wire
Overbody:	Flattened monofilament, 6 lb b.s.
Thorax:	Cock pheasant tail fibres
Wings:	Two turns of badger hackle

177

The USD Black Gnat

This has proved to be a very useful pattern when these small terrestrial flies are blown onto the surface. It, too, is dressed in the upside down style, using a small Pobst Keel Hook. An interesting aspect of this artificial is the method of securing the wing. The wing is formed from polythene sheet, and is secured at the rear by being impaled upon the point of the hook. This makes an extremely durable pattern as the wing is then secured at each end. A further interesting advantage with the polythene sheet is that the under-surface of the wing may be smeared lightly with grease and this, when viewed from below the surface, makes the wings glint and reflect a multitude of colours in a way remarkably similar to that of the natural passing through the outer edges of the window. All in all, this is a very lifelike pattern indeed.

Dressing

Hook:	Size 18 keel hook
Silk:	Black
Body:	Black-dyed cock pheasant centre tail fibre, tied full
Wing:	Clear polythene cut with wing-cutter and trimmed
Hackle:	Black cock

Tying the USD Black Gnat

Take the tying silk down to the bend, and tie in three black-dyed pheasant tail fibres. Now take the silk back to the beginning of the keel, wind a body of the pheasant tail, and tie in. The next stage is a little tricky. Cut one wing only from a sheet of clear polythene and trim the sides in so that they are almost straight, as in the natural. Now place the wing against the hook, and measure the length carefully making sure that there will be sufficient wing protruding over the rear end of the body when the wing is eventually tied in at the front. When you have judged this, impale the wing on the point of the hook, push the hook right through, and work the wing half way round the bend to sit along the top of the body. Only now secure the other end at the eye. Tie in a black cock hackle, wind it, and the job is complete.

The USD Hawthorn

This is similar in design to the new Black Gnat pattern, as again we use an upside-down hook and polythene for the wings. In this case, however, there are two wings and these are tied in flat along the top of the body and slightly apart. The thorax should be dressed very full, and the body picked out well as an aid to flotation.

Tying the USD Hawthorn

Take a number 12 keel hook, run the tying silk down to the bend, and secure there a length of 4 lb monofilament. Secure five or six black ostrich herls and wind up to the eye and tie in. Rib the body herl with the monofilament. Turn the hook upside-down, and trim the body, tapering to the bend. Cut a pair of wings from a sheet of clear polythene, and tie these in on top of the body a third of the way back from the eye. They should be set at a slight angle apart and slightly upwards. Make two long, knotted legs from black-dyed pheasant tail fibres, and tie them in at each side of the thorax, at a slight angle. The last stage is to tie in and wind the black cock hackle, and whip-finish in the normal way.

1 Place a hook upside-down in vice. Secure a length of monofilament at the bend, for use as a rib. Secure five or six black ostrich herls and wind up to the top of the hook's keel.

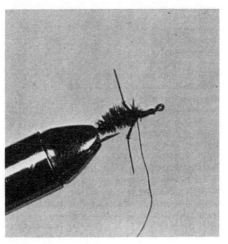

2 Rib body. Trim body with scissors to taper down towards the bend. Tie in two knotted black pheasant tail fibres sloping back under the body, to suggest the trailing legs of the natural fly.

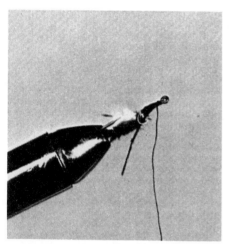

3 Tie in behind the eye two wings cut from clear polythene.

Dressing

Hook:	Size 12 keel hook
Silk:	Black
Rib:	4 lb monofilament
Body:	Five or six black ostrich herls
Wings:	Clear polythene cut with wing-cutter
Hackle:	Black cock hackle
Trailing legs:	Two black-dyed pheasant tail fibres, knotted half-way along

4 Wind a substantial black cock hackle three or four turns behind the eye and in front of the wings. Whip finish and varnish.

5 The finished fly, viewed from above.

The PB Mayfly

This new pattern was an immediate success, and during its first season accounted for many large trout. The body sits down well into the surface film, as does the body of the relatively heavy natural mayfly. Despite this it is an excellent floater even on fast and broken water. It is tied on a keel hook. The plastic body (PB for short) mayfly is a fairly simple pattern to dress if the following instructions are followed.

The three tails are tied well round the bend of the hook and are spread a little apart, using hot orange tying silk. Next, tie in a length of orange firebrand fluorescent floss followed by a length of olive marabou to form a substantial underbody. Rib this underbody *sparsely* with the fluorescent floss, tie in at the eye and trim off excess. Now take a Veniard plastic mayfly body and cut off the very tip of the tapered end to expose a small hole in the hollow body, which can be eased over the eye of the hook. If the correct amount has been trimmed off the plastic body, the exposed hole will be slightly larger than the diameter of the underbody. Ease the plastic body up over the underbody to the tail – but before this is done, a small amount of waterproof glue should be spread around the tail end of the underbody to seal the hole in the plastic. A slit may be made in the other end of the plastic body, so that it can be eased over the eye for securing tightly with several turns of the tying silk, but sufficient room must be left between the end of the plastic body and the eye to tie in the two hackles. The hackles, one olive and one grizzle, can be tied in together.

Dressing

Hook:	Keel long shank, 10 or 12
Silk:	Hot orange
Tails:	Three dark pheasant tail or moose main fibres
Body:	Veniard plastic mayfly
Underbody:	Olive marabou with rib of orange fire-brand fluorescent floss
Hackles:	One each, olive and grizzle

The Super Grizzly

Most of the patterns we have recommended so far have been designed to meet specific needs, or to represent particular species of flies. There are, however, occasions when it is either not necessary to match the hatch, or when you may be unsure just what the trout are eating. At such times a *general* representative pattern comes in useful. Now while there are already many excellent such artificials available, there is always room, as the saying goes, for one more if it is good. This new fly *is* good: it is exceptionally effective, and has proved itself to be a killer on rivers, lakes and mountain streams. It is intended as a general representation of any of the darker-bodied upwinged flies, and although it may be dressed on any size of hook, we have – not surprisingly, perhaps – found that sizes 14 and 16 cover most needs.

The Super Grizzly is a fairly simple pattern to dress. The tying silk of hot orange is taken down to the bend of the hook, where the two tails of muskrat whiskers (or a bunch of fibres for turbulent water) are tied in, spread well apart. Next, tie on three heron herls, twist them together, and wind them up to the eye to form the body. Tie off. The two hackles may now be wound on together, back to back. They should be really good-quality grizzle and red cock, short in the flue and very sharp. To finish the fly, colour the tails pale grey with a felt-tip pen, and then put a dab of varnish at the base of them to ensure they stay apart.

Dressing

Hook:	14 or 16 fine wire U/E
Silk:	Hot orange
Tails:	Several fibres from a pale red dun cock, or muskrat whiskers (for placid water)
Body:	Three heron herls
Hackles:	One each grizzle and red cock tied in together back to back

15 The barbless hook

We want to make at this point an appeal on behalf of the trout.

The use of the barbed hook is almost universal in fly-fishing, and yet we believe that on both practical and aesthetic grounds it could be replaced by the barbless hook tomorrow, and nothing would have been lost. Nothing, perhaps, except by the opponents of angling.

The barbed hook in angling serves two purposes: in many forms of fishing, it does the practical job of helping to keep a bait on the hook. In all forms of fishing – including our own – it serves a second purpose: it gives the angler peace of mind. The thought that a hook is in beyond the barb and *cannot* come out save in the most extreme circumstances, gives the angler a glow inside. It is an insurance policy against him losing fish.

But is it? For several seasons now, we have used barbless hooks – either because we bought them without barbs, or because we have filed off the barbs from our conventional hooks or pressed them flush with tiny pliers – and have found no increase in the numbers of fish we have lost.

Of course, we have lost *some* fish. It is a rare angler indeed who does not lose some fish. But certainly we have not lost *more*, and JG is sure that he has lost far fewer.

How can this be?

The jaw of the trout is for the most part very tough. When the hook with the barb comes unstuck it most often does so because the point has failed to penetrate far enough: the barb just hasn't gone in. If the hook does not simply come away during the fight, a fish is often enough lost for another reason: the immense leverage that is exerted upon the very tip of a hook that has failed to penetrate, causes either the hook to straighten, or for it to snap at its weakest part – at the point where the barb is cut.

With the barbless hook, it may well be the case that the odd fish comes away because the hook slips out. But the barbless hook in normal circumstances goes *in*, every time: there's simply nothing to stop or to slow it. And because any pressure is then exerted upon a fully-sunk point, we do not have our hooks straighten or snap. In fact, neither of us can remember a barbless hook *ever* snapping or being pulled straight. So if the occasional barbless hook does slip out, the balance is more than made up by the advantages outlined above. We do not believe that the barbed hook – and certainly the hook with the enormous barbs of today – lends any practical help in landing a higher proportion of fish.

All of what we have said so far, concerns practical considerations. But there are also aesthetic considerations.

Most experienced fly fishermen would agree that the moment of deception is *the* moment in the practice of their Art: that the rise to the dry fly or the take to the nymph or wet fly is the one moment which provides them with the greatest satisfaction. The hunt and the stalk are exciting, but they are merely the precursors of the cast; the playing and the landing can provide moments of excitement and triumph – but they are moments that are dependent upon the take. It is the *deception* that consummates the skills. And when that moment is achieved, many anglers are content to play the fish out, and then return it.

But before the trout can be returned, the hook has to be removed. And often enough, as every one of us knows, that is not easy. It has to be worried out – sometimes tearing a hole in the fish's mouth, sometimes causing the fish to bleed.

Often enough, when damaged fish are returned to the water, their condition declines, as research in the United States has shown. Frequently, when a bleeding fish goes back, it dies. And what point is there in returning to the water a fish that is doomed to be stunted from that point on, or that is condemned to die?

There is no point at all.

The barbless hook makes all of that unnecessary. It comes out with the merest twist of the fingers. There is little more damage to the trout, than would be caused by a pin-prick in a human. And there is almost *never* bleeding. Indeed, it is often a practical proposition to set the fish free, without ever handling it – and many fish are damaged by the handling alone. By holding the rod far back with one hand, and sliding the other hand down the leader, the trout can often be set free without ever having been taken from the water. This is particularly easy to do – and of particular importance – when returning undersized fish, the sport of tomorrow.

For ourselves we kill very few fish indeed, even sizeable fish. In well-stocked

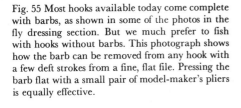

Fig. 55 Most hooks available today come complete with barbs, as shown in some of the photos in the fly dressing section. But we much prefer to fish with hooks without barbs. This photograph shows how the barb can be removed from any hook with a few deft strokes from a fine, flat file. Pressing the barb flat with a small pair of model-maker's pliers is equally effective.

fisheries, where the return of trout is possible (and most often, on still waters in the United Kingdom, the returning of trout is against the rules) we kill little more than a dozen or so fish a year for consumption, from a total of some hundreds caught. On wild fisheries which are not stocked, we kill no fish at all, unless the water will obviously stand the loss, and we very much want one to eat.

Indeed, where circumstances allow, we would support the establishment of special no-kill fisheries – or at least the keeping of parts of fisheries where all undamaged fish could be returned. Certainly, this would make the business of deception more difficult: but it would reduce the burden of stocking costs, and would make the moment of triumph more memorable still, for those who care to pursue it. In practice, it would merely be an extension of the size-limit principle which operates with considerable success, in many of our Northern and Western rain-fed streams. (There is one other point on no-kill fisheries that we would make, and it is this. There is no sense in using a barbless hook, if the trout is condemned to die because of the way it has been played. Many fish die, or suffer from oxygen starvation and brain damage, because the fight has been long drawn out. *Always* play your fish hard – and if they are to go back, get them back as quickly as you are able.)

But let us end on the point of substance.

It is obvious to anyone who walks the banks of our rivers and lakes, and who has the interests of our sport at heart, that much is done in the name of angling that most of us would abhor.

Not the least of our shortcomings as a group is that we do not care as much for our quarry as we might. And those who seek to deny us our sport – and their numbers are even now increasing – will alight on our shortcomings first, when cobbling together their case.

It behoves each of us to raise the standards of behaviour on the bankside, while there is yet time. The avoidance of unnecessary cruelty to fish, however caused, must come right at the top of our list of priorities. And the general introduction of hooks without barbs would be no bad place to begin.

Postscript

At the time of writing this note it is one year since *The Trout and the Fly* was published, and although a second impression has intervened, this third impression is the first opportunity we have had to make any addition at all. In the tiny amount of space that has been made available to us, we want to add, very briefly, a few points which have emerged in that year, in discussions between ourselves as we have continued to observe and experiment.

The following points are listed in random order, with the exception of the first, which is of transcendent importance.

1 The importance of the mirror to the trout (and so to the angler) cannot be overstated. It will emerge and re-emerge through the points which follow. Although the window has been the subject of far more discussion in angling literature, we believe that its importance pales beside that of the mirror, for a trout feeding at the surface. Once the significance of this is grasped, it opens up a new dimension for fly-fisher and fly-dresser alike. The mirror has been the forgotten frontier of the angler's world.

2 Trout which are feeding at the surface appear to the angler to lie level in the water, looking ahead of them, when they are waiting (on a river) for a fly to come into view. There is an implicit assumption in this that if the trout is lying horizontally, it must have its eyes cocked upwards, looking at the surface some distance ahead. We believe this may well not be the case. Instead, we believe that a trout on the look-out for surface food approaching from the mirror may lie at an angle to the surface, with the angle of tilt varying in accordance with the distance ahead and overhead on which the fish is concentrating.

Our observations in the field have appeared to confirm the validity of this belief. However, it can be theorised about as well, for those who prefer meat on the bone.

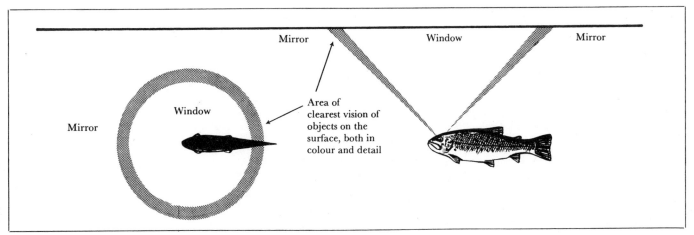

Mirror   Window   Mirror

Mirror

Window

Area of
clearest vision of
objects on the
surface, both in
colour and detail

We will consider the two extreme stages: the angle at which the fish's body is inclined when it takes the fly, and the the angle from which it might start off on its ascent.

The first is the easier to deal with. We have photographed many trout which have broken the surface with their nebs at the moment of taking the fly. Without exception, these photographs have shown the neb of the fish pointing into the air at a very steep angle to the surface, while the body of the fish below water appears to lie at the shallow angle to the surface at which the angler is accustomed to seeing it. The photograph on page 94 illustrates the point perfectly – and the difference between the real angle indicated by the head of the fish, and the apparent angle of the body in the water, must obviously be accounted for by refraction.

The evidence for the fish being angled even before he begins his ascent, in spite of appearances, is circumstantial but interesting – with again, of course, any difference between actual angle and perceived horizontal position again being accounted for by refraction.

While a trout can see with one eye, it can judge distances only by looking with both eyes. The trout focusses by moving its lens towards and away from its retina. Because the lens is dependent for movement on a ligament which cannot retract but whose position is known, and a muscle which can retract and the position of which is also known, the direction of travel of the lens towards the retina can be established. This direction, we understand, is consistent with the fish receiving it clearest image towards the back of the retina: the direction in which the image would apparently be transmitted through the lens if the fish were looking forwards.

For a fish to look directly forward with both eyes at an object or area, it must point its body in the direction it wishes to look; it just doesn't have a neck to enable it to do anything else. And if that object or area is the water surface, the fish presumably must point its body towards the surface: in other words, it seems it must lie with its body angled upwards, towards the surface, when on the look-out for surface food.

3 We have already mentioned that at least in many cases, a fish is inclined at a very steep angle when it accepts a fly from the water surface. We do not know exactly what this angle is, but it is interesting to speculate. We suspect that it is of the order of 50 degrees to the vertical. We believe this to be the case because we already know that the fish gets its clearest and most detailed view of the fly insofar as light is concerned, when the fly is just on the inside edge of the window. And we also already know that he will get his best view insofar as his eyes are concerned by looking straight ahead with both eyes.

As interception of a surface fly calls for fine judgment, we believe that the trout will instinctively make use of every facility available to him – through both light and eye. In other words, in the final stages of the rise it is probable that he looks at the edge of his window with both eyes looking directly forward: and he can do that only by pointing his head and body at it. Light comes to his eye from the edge of his window at around 48 degrees to the vertical and it therefore seems probable that he aligns his body roughly along this path.

4 The mirror at night is pitch dark. We have shown through our photographs just how easily the trout can see the spinner at sunset and in moonlight, when looking up towards the mirror – even though that same fly is invisible to the angler looking down. What happens is that the spreadeagled, transparent wings of the fly allow what light there is to pass through them – and so they appear as small pools of light in the otherwise total darkness of the mirror all around.

Extending the same principle to flylines, a floating line of any kind or colour is visible to the fish at night if that line is lying in the surface film and is moved. It refracts some light down from around its sides, and any disturbance the line makes is clearly evident. (It is also true that at night the lighter in colour a line is, the more noticeable it is, whether moved or not.)

There are several implications in all of this. A number of writers have noted that sea-trout being fished for at night become more difficult to catch when the moon is behind the angler: the reason, they have said, is because the silhouetted angler casts shadows down the pool into the window of the trout. This may indeed be the case. But we believe it just as likely that the fish are difficult to catch for a different or supplementary reason. If the moon is behind the angler from the position of the fish, then it is behind the line as well. And if the line is on the surface and moved, then it will create an alarming herring-bone light pattern in the darkness of the mirror that the trout or sea-trout can see.

5 Nylon floating on the surface allows light – much after the manner of spreadeagled spinners' wings – to pass through it. If clear nylon is used on the surface at night, the light passing through it will appear like a bright crack in the darkness of the mirror: a crack which runs right up to any surface fly being fished! There are obvious lessons in this not just for the fly-fisher (keep your leader as well-sunk at night as you do during the day) – but for the coarse angler as well – particularly for anglers who freeline floating bread to carp at night.

6 We have carried out exhaustive tests on different-coloured leaders on and below the surface in conditions ranging from noon-day sun to dark night. While the ideal leader will obviously be one dyed to the colour the mirror is reflecting from the bottom over any given area of bed, we have found that a leader dyed brown is the least obtrusive over the widest range of conditions. A black leader, as might be expected, is least visible against the mirror at night. Again, all leaders are less visible below the surface at night, just as they are during the day – again something it might be helpful for carp anglers and others to note.

7 It has nothing to do with refraction, but trout in chalk-streams cannot see nearly as far as some fly-fishers would believe. The water looks gin-clear when illuminated by the sun, and viewed from above. But the trout must

look horizontally through the water, and all the billions of particles of suspended chalk reflect light back to him. The effect, as we have seen demonstrated by a ciné-camera sunk into the river-bed, and pointed horizontally, is very much like switching on one's car headlights in a fog. Under some circumstances, chalk-stream trout cannot see more than 2–3 ft. Under many circumstances, chalk-stream trout cannot see more than 4–5 ft. Even in the clearest and shallowest chalk-stream, under the most favourable light conditions, it is doubtful if the fish can see 10 ft through the water. These observations are not, of course, valid for trout in very clear lakes, wherein there is no flow to disturb and carry sediment. Nor do we believe it invalidates the photograph and caption of BC on page 87: that photograph was taken in water which was scarcely moving.

8 The dressings of the USD dun and spinner were designed to reproduce as near-exactly as possible the precise optical effects presented to the trout by natural flies. However, we have found through further experimentation that the hooking properties of the dun can be improved by replacing the cut-hackle wings with a few calf-tail fibres; and the hooking properties of the spinners can be improved by tying them exactly as described but on standard hooks for broken water; and on standard hooks without any parachute hackle at all, on smooth water. Dressed in this last way, where it can be fished, this spinner dressing is deadly.

Brian Clarke
John Goddard
February, 1981

Index